Organized Labour and Politics in Mexico
Changes, Continuities and Contradictions

Graciela Bensusán and Kevin J. Middlebrook

INSTITUTE FOR THE STUDY OF THE
AMERICAS

UNIVERSITY OF LONDON · SCHOOL OF ADVANCED STUDY

© Institute for the Study of the Americas, University of London, 2012

British Library Cataloguing-in-Publication Data
A catalogue record for this book is available from the British Library

ISBN 978 0 9567549 2 9

INSTITUTE FOR THE STUDY OF THE
A M E R I C A S
UNIVERSITY OF LONDON · SCHOOL OF ADVANCED STUDY

Institute for the Study of the Americas
School of Advanced Study
University of London
Senate House
London WC1E 7HU

Telephone: 020 7862 8870
Fax: 020 7862 8886

Email: americas@sas.ac.uk
Web: www.americas.sas.ac.uk

Contents

List of Tables

Acronyms

AFL-CIO	American Federation of Labor-Congress of Industrial Organizations
ANAD	Asociación Nacional de Abogados Democráticos/National Association of Democratic Lawyers
BO	Banco Obrero/Worker Bank
CCE	Consejo Coordinador Empresarial/Private Sector Coordinating Council
CEDAW	Convention on the Elimination of All Forms of Discrimination Against Women
CFE	Comisión Federal de Electricidad/Federal Electrical Commission
CIPM	Coordinadora Inter-sindical Primero de Mayo/May 1 Inter-Union Coordinating Network
CNDH	Comisión Nacional de Derechos Humanos/National Human Rights Commission
CNSM	Comisión Nacional de los Salarios Mínimos/National Minimum Wage Commission
CNTE	Coordinadora Nacional de Trabajadores de la Educación/National Coordinating Committee of Education Workers
COM	Casa del Obrero Mundial/House of the World Worker
COPARMEX	Confederación Patronal de la República Mexicana/Mexican Employers' Confederation
CROC	Confederación Revolucionaria de Obreros y Campesinos/Revolutionary Confederation of Workers and Peasants
CROM	Confederación Regional Obrera Mexicana/Mexican Regional Labour Confederation
CT	Congreso del Trabajo/Labour Congress
CTM	Confederación de Trabajadores de México/Confederation of Mexican Workers
CUSWA	United Steelworkers in Canada
EAP	economically active population
FAT	Frente Auténtico del Trabajo/Authentic Labour Front
FDSSP	Federación Democrática de Sindicatos de Servidores Públicos/Democratic Federation of Public Service Workers' Unions
FESEBS	Federación de Sindicatos de Empresas de Bienes y Servicios/Federation of Unions of Goods and Services Enterprises
FSM	Frente Sindical Mexicano/Mexican Union Front
FSTSE	Federación de Sindicatos de Trabajadores al Servicio del Estado/Federation of Public Service Workers' Unions

GDP	gross domestic product
ICFTU	International Confederation of Free Trade Unions
ILO	International Labour Organization
IMF	International Metalworkers' Federation
IMSS	Instituto Mexicano del Seguro Social/Mexican Social Security Institute
INEGI	Instituto Nacional de Estadística, Geografía e Informática/National Institute of Statistics, Geography and Informatics
ISSSTE	Instituto de Seguridad y Servicios Sociales de los Trabajadores del Estado/Social Security Institute for State Workers
JFCA	Junta Federal de Conciliación y Arbitraje/Federal Conciliation and Arbitration Board
JLCA	Junta Local de Conciliación y Arbitraje/Local Conciliation and Arbitration Board
LFC	Luz y Fuerza del Centro/Central Light and Power
LFT	Ley Federal del Trabajo/Federal Labour Law
LFTSE	Ley Federal de los Trabajadores al Servicio del Estado/Federal Law for Public Service Workers
NAALC	North American Agreement on Labor Cooperation
NAFTA	North American Free Trade Agreement
NAO	national administrative office
NGO	non-governmental organization
PAN	Partido Acción Nacional/National Action Party
PANAL	Partido Nueva Alianza/New Alliance Party
PRD	Partido de la Revolución Democrática/Party of the Democratic Revolution
PRI	Partido Revolucionario Institucional/Institutional Revolutionary Party
PT	Partido del Trabajo/Labour Party
PVEM	Partido Verde Ecologista de México/Mexican Ecologist Green Party
RMALC	Red Mexicana de Acción frente al Libre Comercio/Mexican Action Network Against Free Trade
SAR	Sistema de Ahorro para el Retiro/Retirement Saving System
SCMW	Support Committee for Maquiladora Workers
SME	Sindicato Mexicano de Electricistas/Mexican Electricians' Union
SNTE	Sindicato Nacional de Trabajadores de la Educación/National Education Workers' Union
SNTMMSRM	Sindicato Nacional de Trabajadores Mineros, Metalúrgicos y Similares de la República Mexicana/Mexican Mining and Metalworkers' Union
SNTSS	Sindicato Nacional de Trabajadores del Seguro Social/National Union of Social Security Workers
STIMAHCS	Sindicato de Trabajadores en la Industria Metálica, Acero, Hierro, Conexos y Similares/Union of Workers in the Metal, Iron, Steel and Related and Similar Industries
STPRM	Sindicato de Trabajadores Petroleros de la República Mexicana/Mexican Petroleum Workers' Union

STPS   Secretaría del Trabajo y Previsión Social/Ministry of Labour and
            Social Welfare
STRM   Sindicato de Telefonistas de la República Mexicana/Mexican
            Telephone Workers' Union
TELMEX   Teléfonos de México/Mexican Telephone Company
UAW   United Automobile, Aerospace, and Agricultural Implement Workers
            of America
UE   United Electrical, Radio, and Machine Workers of America
UNT   Unión Nacional de Trabajadores/National Union of Workers
USWA   United Steelworkers of America
WCL   World Confederation of Labour

About the Authors

Graciela Bensusán is Research Professor at the Universidad Autónoma Metropolitana-Xochimilco in Mexico City, a post she has held since 1976. Since 1989 she has also been Professor (part-time) at the Facultad Latinoamericana de Ciencias Sociales-México. She holds a law degree from the Facultad de Derecho y Ciencias Sociales at the Universidad de Buenos Aires and a PhD in political science from the Facultad de Ciencias Políticas y Sociales at the Universidad Nacional Autónoma de México. Professor Bensusán is a member of Mexico's Sistema Nacional de Investigadores (Level III) and the Academia Mexicana de Ciencias. She has also held research appointments at the Facultad de Ciencias Políticas y Sociales, Universidad Nacional Autónoma de México; the Comisión Económica para América Latina y el Caribe in Santiago, Chile; and, at the University of London, the Institute for the Study of the Americas and King's College.

Professor Bensusán is author or co-author of four books, including *El modelo mexicano de regulación laboral* (2000), and editor or co-editor of ten books, including *Diseño legal y desempeño real: instituciones laborales en América Latina* (2006), *Integración regional y relaciones industriales en América del Norte* (1996) and *Negociación y conflicto laboral en México* (1992). Her co-edited book *Trabajo y trabajadores en el México contemporáneo* (2000) won the Latin American Studies Association Labor Section's book prize in 2001. In addition, she has published 130 book chapters and articles in such journals as *Estudios Sociológicos, Relations Industrielles, Revista Latinoamericana de Estudios del Trabajo, Revista Mexicana de Sociología, Revista Perfiles Latinoamericanos* and *Revista Sociológica*.

Professor Bensusán has held numerous research grants from Mexico's Consejo Nacional de Ciencia y Tecnología, the Comisión Económica para América Latina y el Caribe, the Fundación Friedrich Ebert, the International Labour Organization and other public and private funding agencies. Her current research focuses on the comparative analysis of labour policies, institutions and organizations in Latin America.

Her extensive professional activities have included membership on the editorial boards of *Labor Studies Journal, Revista Gestión y Política, Revista Internacional del Trabajo, Revista Mexicana de Sociología* and *Revista Perfiles*

Latinoamericanos, as well as membership on the social science review panel of Mexico's Sistema Nacional de Investigadores.

Kevin J. Middlebrook is Professor of Politics at the Institute for the Study of the Americas, University of London. Between 1995 and 2001 he was Director of the Center for U.S.-Mexican Studies at the University of California-San Diego, where he also held an appointment as Adjunct Professor of Political Science. Educated at Harvard University, he has held postdoctoral fellowships at the Center for U.S.-Mexican Studies and the Hoover Institution on War, Revolution, and Peace at Stanford University, as well as research grants from the Fulbright-Hays Commission, the Howard Heinz Endowment, the Nuffield Foundation and the Social Science Research Council.

Professor Middlebrook is the author of *The Paradox of Revolution: Labor, the State, and Authoritarianism in Mexico* (1995), winner of the 1996 Hubert Herring Book Prize from the Pacific Coast Council of Latin American Studies, and co-author of *Mexico since 1980: A Second Revolution in Economics, Politics, and Society* (2008). He is also editor or co-editor of nine books, including *Confronting Development: Assessing Mexico's Economic and Social Policy Challenges* (2003) and *Dilemmas of Political Change in Mexico* (2004). In addition, he has published numerous chapters in edited books and articles in, among other journals, *Comparative Politics, Estudios Sociológicos, Foro Internacional, Journal of Latin American Studies, Latin American Research Review, Revista Mexicana de Sociología* and *World Politics*.

Professor Middlebrook's current research focuses on transnational worker rights coalitions and the performance of the labour institutions created in association with the North American Free Trade Agreement, with particular attention to the lessons that these institutions offer for an assessment of alternative strategies for the international defence of workers' rights.

His extensive professional activities include membership on the editorial boards of the *Journal of Latin American Studies* and the *Latin American Research Review*. He was the Latin American Studies Association's (LASA) first elected Treasurer (2006–10), and he is co-founder and co-chair of LASA's organized section on Mexico (2009–12).

Acknowledgements

The authors wish to thank Gabriela Medina for her excellent research assistance in the preparation of this book, and Francisco Flores-Macias for his talented statistical analysis of the survey data examined in Chapter Three. Ilán Bizberg, Katrina Burgess and Jonathan Fox generously offered insightful comments on the manuscript. The publications team (Kerry Whitston, Valerie Hall and Emily Morrell) at the School of Advanced Study, University of London, oversaw the final production process with efficiency and professionalism.

The authors acknowledge the publisher's permission to draw material from their chapter 'Organized Labor and Politics' in Roderic Ai Camp (ed.), *The Oxford Handbook of Mexican Politics* (New York: Oxford University Press, 2012).

The cover image is an untitled pencil drawing by Diego Rivera from the early 1930s; the photograph is by Kat Hannon. The authors are grateful to the Instituto Nacional de Bellas Artes and the Fideicomiso Diego Rivera y Frida Kahlo for permission to reproduce the image here. Reproduction authorized by the Instituto Nacional de Bellas Artes y Literatura, 2012; all rights reserved © 2012 Banco de México, fiduciary for the Museos Diego Rivera y Frida Kahlo.

Unless otherwise noted, all translations of material originally written in Spanish are by the authors. Monetary values given in both Mexican pesos and US dollars were converted at the contemporaneous exchange rate.

The authors alone are responsible for any omissions or errors of fact or interpretation.

Chapter One
Introduction

Organized labour served as a pillar of the post-revolutionary authoritarian regime that held sway in Mexico from the 1920s through the 1990s. Beginning in the 1980s, however, extensive market-liberalizing reforms undermined the economic bases of the alliance between labour and the ruling political elite. Economic restructuring in the public and private sectors sharply reduced unions' bargaining leverage over wages, fringe benefits and working conditions. As a consequence, the unionized share of the economically active population (EAP) declined significantly and workers' income fell. As traditional, government-allied unions lost support, the overarching Labour Congress (Congreso del Trabajo, CT) splintered. The emergence of more independent labour organizations increased political pluralism in the labour movement, and the consolidation of multiparty electoral competition after the mid-1990s expanded individual workers' choices at the ballot box. Nevertheless, most unions remained dominated by leaders whose entrenched position was underpinned by labour law provisions that effectively blocked rank-and-file efforts to hold them accountable. This same legal regime granted government officials extensive controls over both the formation of unions and their actions (including strikes), thereby providing the government with significant capacity to mediate redistributive conflicts. The combination of weakened labour organizations, unaccountable union leadership and strong state controls on union activities fundamentally constrained workers' capacity to defend their interests.

It is not surprising that far-reaching economic restructuring in Mexico adversely affected the organized labour movement; parallel processes of market-liberalizing reform have had similar effects on unionized workers in many countries.[1] Nor is it remarkable that organized labour exercised limited influence over the terms or impact of economic liberalization. The defining characteristics of the political context in which economic opening occurred during the 1980s and early 1990s — a division of constitutional authority

---

1   See, among other works, Burgess, 2004; Kurtz, 2004, pp. 271–3, 297–8; Roberts, 1998, pp. 65–7; Visser, 2006.

that gave the federal executive substantial latitude to define (and redefine) national economic policy, the continued electoral and legislative dominance of the 'official', state-subsidized Institutional Revolutionary Party (Partido Revolucionario Institucional, PRI) and the governing elite's capacity to limit mass demands through a combination of legal controls and an extensive network of state-society alliances dating to the 1920s and 1930s — greatly reduced the ability of popular groups to influence national policy debates so as to define a more inclusive economic strategy.[2]

In exchange for backing the heterodox macroeconomic 'stabilization pacts' that the government adopted to manage the devastating effects of Mexico's post-1982 debt crisis, leading elements of the state-subsidized, 'official' labour movement did win limited policy concessions that gave marginal protection to their own members. Moreover, wage earners in general certainly benefited greatly from economic policy makers' success in controlling inflation after the late 1980s. In a few instances, unions in strategic sectors (telecommunications, for example) also managed to negotiate comparatively favourable terms for the privatization of state-owned enterprises. For the most part, however, economic restructuring cost workers heavily in terms of reduced earnings, cutbacks in company-provided fringe benefits, diminished employment opportunities in the formal sector and sharply curtailed influence in the workplace. Given the combination of strong state administrative controls over strikes and other forms of labour protest, the resilience of the historic alliance between the PRI and the country's most important labour organizations, the constrained bargaining capacity of many unions and their limited tradition of mobilization after the late 1940s, and the general weakness of workplace-level representational arrangements that would permit rank-and-file union members to hold their leaders accountable, these outcomes were quite predictable.[3]

However, the Mexican case is more puzzling — and therefore of particular interest in the comparative study of labour and politics — in two important respects: labour's response to regime democratization, and the impact of political democratization on state-labour relations. Contrary to some predictions (Valenzuela, 1989, p. 463), the triumph of the centre-right National Action Party (Partido Acción Nacional, PAN) over the labour movement's

2   For a more detailed discussion of the politics of economic restructuring in Mexico, see Middlebrook and Zepeda, 2003, pp. 10–16. The January 1994 revolt led by the Zapatista Army of National Liberation (Ejército Zapatista de Liberación Nacional) in the southern state of Chiapas did, however, quickly lay to rest the view that Mexico's liberalizing reformers had engineered a broad programme of economic restructuring without provoking major political or social upheavals.

3   In her comparative analysis of labour-based parties' responses to the challenges posed by economic liberalization, Burgess (2004, pp. 6–7) argued that the Mexican labour movement collaborated with market-liberalizing reforms mainly in order to preserve its alliance with the PRI.

historic partisan ally, the PRI, in the 2000 presidential election did not lead to intensified strike action or protracted political conflict. It was perhaps reasonable to anticipate a different response to partisan alternation in power at the national level because the leadership of the 'official' labour movement had vigorously resisted regime opening since the mid-1970s.[4] Organized labour's weakened overall position may have somewhat limited its effective capacity to challenge the incoming PAN government. Nonetheless, the administration of newly elected President Vicente Fox Quesada (2000–06) did consider labour disruption by PRI-affiliated unions a very real threat.

The Fox administration's decision to adopt a conciliatory attitude toward PRI-allied unions no doubt helped avoid any major political clash. However, the core factor underpinning the calculations of labour leaders and government officials alike was the established state-labour relations regime — that is, the array of legal provisions, judicial precedents and informal practices and procedures governing state-labour interactions, including those shaping the formation, actions and internal life of worker organizations. Any labour attempt at confrontation would have faced significant obstacles in the legal controls that government officials wield over strikes and other forms of worker mobilization, backed up by the state's monopoly on the use of force. At the same time, serious conflict with the PAN government might have jeopardized the various legal and administrative subsidies that sustain the entrenched leaders of many unions. In short, the political pragmatism that characterized the actions of both the labour movement and the Fox administration during Mexico's democratic transition in 2000 rested on the state-labour relations regime forged in the decades following the Mexican Revolution.

In stressing the importance of the established labour relations regime as an explanation for organized labour's response to political change in Mexico after 2000, we engage the broader debate in comparative politics regarding the role of labour movements in democratization. Levitsky and Mainwaring (2006) have demonstrated that the stances labour movements adopted toward democracy in twentieth-century Latin America were far more varied than previous accounts have suggested.[5] On the basis of a comparative examination

4   Indeed, despite nearly two decades of economic reversals under PRI-led governments, a plurality of unionized voters still cast their ballots for the PRI's presidential candidate in 2000. See Chapter Three.

5   Rueschemeyer, Stephens and Stephens (1992) famously argued that the working class has been a crucial — and historically quite consistent — force in favour of political democracy because 'those who have only to gain from democracy will be its most reliable promoters and defenders' (p. 57). Like other analysts of labour's role in democratic transitions (see especially Valenzuela, 1989), these authors did recognize some exceptions to their argument. They noted that 'exceptions to the pro-democratic posture of the working class occurred where the class was initially mobilized by . . . a hegemonic party linked to the state apparatus', and they acknowledged that 'the conditions under which the social construction of working-class interests takes a non-democratic form — as it did in Leninism [—]' merit special attention

of nine Latin American countries (Argentina, Bolivia, Brazil, Chile, Colombia, Mexico, Nicaragua, Peru and Venezuela) over the 1945–2000 period, they concluded that although labour movements often contributed significantly to successful struggles to establish political democracy, in several instances they either supported extra-constitutional challenges to elected governments or pursued maximalist strategies that undercut democratic regimes. Levitsky and Mainwaring especially emphasized the historical importance of cases in which labour movements strongly supported inclusionary authoritarian regimes, such as those in Argentina (1946–55), Nicaragua (1979–90), Peru (1969–77) and of course Mexico.

In their attempt to account for variation in labour support for democracy, Levitsky and Mainwaring argued (2006, p. 21) that the political orientation of labour movements in twentieth-century Latin America depended primarily on two factors: the character of their alliances with political parties (and whether labour's party allies firmly supported democracy or adopted merely instrumental positions concerning democratic or authoritarian rule), and the perceived regime alternatives. These are certainly important considerations. However, on the basis of these elements alone, one would have predicted that the bulk of the Mexican labour movement — long allied with the PRI and facing a new PAN government with historically strong ties to the private sector — would have mobilized against the Fox administration.[6] Thus certainly in the Mexican case, and perhaps in democratic transitions from other inclusionary authoritarian regimes as well, privileging labour-party ties led Levitsky and Mainwaring to overlook the state-labour relations regime as an important additional variable in shaping labour's stance regarding democratization.

We emphasize that it is the labour relations **regime** (and not merely selected public policies regarding such labour-related issues as wages or social welfare benefits) that is the focus of discussion here. Levitsky and Mainwaring observed

(pp. 8, 59). Mexico was the principal empirical referent that they offered in support of these points. Nevertheless, Rueschemeyer, Stephens and Stephens stopped well short of suggesting that post-revolutionary authoritarian regimes like Mexico before 2000 might constitute a general class of exceptions to their argument concerning labour's historically consistent support for democratization. For an early critique of their position and a comparative analysis of the Mexican, Nicaraguan and Russian cases, see Middlebrook, 1997.

6   There is some ambiguity in Levitsky and Mainwaring's presentation regarding whether a labour movement's predicted defence of an inclusionary authoritarian regime applies only to initial phases of regime liberalization or to subsequent stages of democratization. It is entirely logical that both union leaders and rank-and-file members would continue to support a regime that had provided them with substantial material, organizational or symbolic rewards, especially if the prospective transition to a more procedurally democratic alternative centred on a political party with a well-known antipathy to labour. But as a democratic transition accelerates, the labour movement may find it increasingly impractical to mobilize strongly in favour of the *ancien régime*, especially if the transition is marked by the defeat of its principal partisan ally in a free and fair election.

that inclusionary authoritarian regimes frequently offer labour movements a wide range of material, organizational, political and symbolic benefits, and that labour movements (particularly their leaders, who may enjoy substantial latitude to define the positions that unions adopt toward democratization) view with considerable scepticism, if not overt hostility, the prospect that these gains might be endangered by regime change. However, in stressing that a newly installed democratic government might adopt less labour-friendly policies, Levitsky and Mainwaring implied that democratization may jeopardize accumulated labour benefits more immediately than may actually be the case. If many of the prerogatives that the labour movement enjoys are highly institutionalized, even an arch-conservative democratic government may find it difficult to enact radical reforms in short order.[7] Under such circumstances, the labour movement's initial response to democratization may be much less confrontational than Levitsky and Mainwaring suggested.[8]

The second puzzling aspect of labour and democratization in contemporary Mexico is that intense multiparty electoral competition and partisan alternation in power at both federal and state levels have not yet produced a more significant transformation of the state-labour relations regime. After all, in a more fully democratic political environment characterized by much lower levels of political repression and substantially reduced presidential powers, labour organizations in principle have increased opportunities to pressure for the removal of legal controls on union formation and strikes, as well as to hold government officials more directly accountable for their administration of labour law. Yet, despite some important gains (especially via judicial rulings that have blocked some particularly controversial government actions toward individual unions, challenged existing controls on freedom of association and somewhat strengthened the procedural bases for more active rank-and-file participation in internal union affairs), the overall changes in Mexico's state-labour relations regime since 2000 have been remarkably modest.

This surprising — and, for those who have promoted the reform of the labour relations regime as a key part of broader societal democratization, disappointing — outcome reflects a combination of factors. Up until the brief national debate about labour law reform that occurred in March–April 2011, none of the principal parties represented in the national Congress had made reform of the Federal Labour Law (Ley Federal del Trabajo, LFT) an

---

7   It is telling in this regard that, despite far-reaching economic policy changes in Latin America since the 1980s, few elected governments have significantly reformed their national labour laws. See Inter-American Development Bank, 1997, p. 46, figure 27; Ciudad, 2002, pp. 9–11; Stallings and Peres, 2000, p. 43.

8   Considerations such as a labour movement's tradition of militant action (or lack thereof) and the degree of political competition among different labour factions may also have a significant impact on labour's response to the possible challenges posed by democratic regime change.

especially high priority. This stance may have reflected in part the reduced electoral significance of the unionized population and the relative weakness of (and political divisions among) those unions and allied parties most committed to democratizing key aspects of state-labour relations. At the same time, old-guard labour organizations have mounted a dogged defence of their legal and institutional prerogatives, which has raised the political costs of pursuing progressive legal reforms. Equally important, however, parties across the entire partisan spectrum have found political advantage in preserving the institutional controls on worker participation that are embedded in the established labour relations regime.

The failure to enact a progressive reform of the Federal Labour Law, or to effect a more general transformation of state-labour relations, has had momentous consequences for both the labour movement and for Mexican society more generally. As we have already noted, state administrative controls on labour and the relative weakness of democratically organized trade unions have sharply constrained workers' capacity to advance their interests during a period of far-reaching economic and political change. On a broad array of issues — ranging from the terms of industrial restructuring in the workplace, to the setting of national wage and social welfare policies, to debates about how to configure an overall national economic strategy that promotes more socially equitable development — the labour movement has a potentially significant role to play. In many historical contexts, the actions of trade unions have helped raise skill and employment standards and reduce socio-economic inequalities (Freeman and Medoff, 1984; Aidt and Tzannatos, 2002; Hayter and Weinberg, 2011). In Mexico, however, the authentic voice of unionized workers has largely been silenced by legal restrictions and by the inertia of unaccountable or spurious labour leaders whose position is sustained by a labour relations regime inherited from the country's authoritarian past.

This book, then, examines the changes, continuities and contradictions characterizing labour politics in Mexico since the 1980s. Because of the significance of the established labour relations regime for developments affecting the organized labour movement during this period, Chapter Two overviews the state-labour relations regime that was institutionalized in the years following the Mexican Revolution of 1910–20. In particular, it argues that political leaders seeking to mediate workers' participation in national affairs forged both legal and administrative arrangements to regulate the social relations of capitalist production and a political alliance with leading elements of an emerging labour movement. These reinforcing strategies — the first centred on the state apparatus, the second eventually centred on an 'official' governing party — permitted the ruling political elite to control working-class mobilization, limit political and organizational pluralism in the labour movement and restrain workers' demands, elements that together underpinned post-revolutionary authoritarian rule in Mexico.[9]

Of these two strategies, it has been the organized labour movement's durable alliance with a post-revolutionary 'official' party that has most commonly drawn the attention of analysts of Mexican labour politics. After 1938, the Confederation of Mexican Workers (Confederación de Trabajadores de México, CTM), the country's largest and most politically influential labour confederation, served as the PRI's official labour sector. This arrangement powerfully symbolized labour's inclusion in the post-revolutionary governing coalition. Union leaders' ties to the 'official' party also provided them with a share (however modest) of political power and the capacity to influence some government decisions on issues affecting workers, as well as much-valued opportunities for individual political mobility (and, in many instances, illicit personal enrichment) via PRI candidacies for elective office at the federal, state and municipal levels.[10] Because of tight links between the 'official' party and the state and the party's political hegemony from the 1930s into the 1990s, some analysts concluded that party-labour ties constituted the principal means through which the governing political elite subordinated labour.[11]

The 'official' party certainly played a key part in sustaining mass support for Mexico's post-revolutionary regime. From the 1930s until the 1980s, the PRI and its predecessor organizations[12] embodied both nationalist sentiment and ideological support for active state intervention in socio-economic affairs to achieve the revolution's redistributive goals, positions that coincided closely with the aspirations of many working-class organizations. The prospect of personal political rewards in the form of PRI candidacies (which, during the long period of 'official' party hegemony, effectively guaranteed election to the post in question) may also have encouraged leaders of some government-allied unions to moderate their demands.

However, the PRI and its predecessors were designed first and foremost as broadly inclusive bodies responsible for coalescing as diverse an array of

---

9   On the concept of post-revolutionary authoritarianism and the Mexican case, see Middlebrook, 1995, chapter 1.

10 On the importance of corruption in maintaining Mexico's post-revolutionary political order, see Blum, 1997 and Morris, 1999.

11 See, for example, Smith, 1979, pp. 49–62, and Collier and Collier, 1991, pp. 202, 416–9.

12 Mexico's 'official' party was founded in 1929 as the Revolutionary National Party (Partido Nacional Revolucionario), with the goal of curtailing factional rivalries and political instability by uniting in a single body all 'revolutionary' forces emerging from the country's 1910–20 revolution. It was restructured as the Party of the Mexican Revolution (Partido de la Revolución Mexicana) in 1938 on the basis of labour, peasant, military and 'popular' sectors. The military sector was formally eliminated in 1940 and became part of the popular sector after the latter was reorganized in 1943. Further internal reforms were effected in 1946, and the party was renamed the Institutional Revolutionary Party (PRI).

interests as possible, a task facilitated by the diffuseness of post-revolutionary political ideas. The party itself had limited organizational autonomy vis-à-vis the state and lacked the institutional capacity to block political mobilization or otherwise exercise direct control over affiliated groups. Organized labour, which held significant economic bargaining leverage and some independent capacity for collective action, traditionally enjoyed considerable autonomy within the party framework. At root, then, elite control over lower-class actors in post-revolutionary Mexico ultimately rested on state power. In assessing the relative importance of party-based and state-based elements of political control, the fact that extensive legal and administrative controls on labour participation remained in place following the PRI's defeat in Mexico's 2000 presidential election clearly demonstrates the enduring significance of the latter.

This overview of the state-labour relations regime lays the basis for an examination in Chapter Three of the impact of economic restructuring and electoral democratization on organized labour. After the mid-1980s Mexico underwent dual economic and political transformations. However, economic reform proceeded much more rapidly than the country's political opening. Indeed, the speed and relative ease with which government decision makers adopted market-liberalizing economic measures were due largely to the dominating power of the federal executive, strong state controls on strikes and other forms of mobilization by mass actors such as organized labour and, more generally, the limited capacity of popular groups to protest actions that harmed their material interests. In the labour sector, the consequences of radical economic restructuring and a pro-business shift in government policies included a sharp, sustained fall in the inflation-adjusted value of minimum wages and average incomes, reduced employment opportunities in the formal sector of the economy, cuts in employer-provided fringe benefits, declining union influence over production processes and growing numbers of 'ghost unions' and 'employer protection contracts' that defended employer prerogatives in the workplace. The unionization rate also declined substantially and, under the pressure of deteriorating economic circumstances, the labour movement suffered increasing organizational fragmentation — and with it, a further erosion of its political influence.

Chapter Three also examines in detail the impact of electoral democratization on the organized labour movement. As noted above, from the mid-1970s onward the CTM systematically opposed both the liberalization of Mexico's post-revolutionary regime and internal PRI reforms that threatened to weaken the influence of traditional sectoral organizations in party decision making. Over time, however, open, multiparty competition for office gradually displaced closed sectoral manoeuvring over PRI candidacies as the central focus of electoral politics in Mexico. This change produced significant political losses for the CTM and many other government-allied labour organizations. Although 'official' unions managed to preserve their control over sectoral-representation positions in many tripartite public bodies (those whose governing or advisory councils include business, government and labour representatives), their share of labour representation in the federal Chamber of Deputies fell sharply. Among nationally important labour organizations, only the National Education Workers' Union (Sindicato Nacional de Trabajadores de la Educación, SNTE) managed to expand substantially its political presence and policy influence after the PRI's historic defeat in the 2000 presidential election.

One important consequence of electoral democratization was that rank-and-file union members gained expanded scope for individual political choice. Especially after the mid-1990s, institutional reforms ensuring free and fair electoral processes made it increasingly difficult for union leaders to control their members' behaviour at the polls. Nevertheless, members of union households were still more likely to identify with the PRI than with any other party, and opinion poll data indicate that in the year 2000 union households voted for the PRI's presidential candidate in significantly greater numbers than non-union households. Over the 2000–06 period, however, the proportion of PRI identifiers fell at the same time that the share of PAN identifiers rose, and in the 2006 presidential election a higher proportion of union households reported supporting the PAN's victorious candidate than the PRI's candidate.

Chapter Four analyses the labour policies adopted by the administrations of President Vicente Fox and President Felipe Calderón Hinojosa (2006–12), including their attempts at federal labour law reform and their handling of high-profile conflicts with unions representing miners and electrical power workers. The failure of Mexico's transitional government to adopt progressive labour law reforms was a major setback for broader processes of democratization, and it marked a generally more conservative shift in the Fox administration's labour policies as PAN officials, like their PRI predecessors, acknowledged their dependence on old-style labour leaders' willingness to control rank-and-file demands in exchange for continued government support. In turn, protracted conflicts involving mining and electrical power workers demonstrated the ways in which the preservation of Mexico's established state-labour relations regime permitted government officials — even in a formally democratic context — to undercut elected union leaders and pursue policies that conspicuously benefited their big-business allies.

Chapter Five examines the ways in which the economic and political transformations of the 1980s and 1990s have altered the power resources available to Mexican labour organizations. In particular, it analyses the transnational alliances that some politically independent unions have forged with their Canadian and US counterparts since the early 1990s and their use of international forums to defend labour rights in Mexico. The two most important such forums have been the institutions created in 1994 by the North American Agreement on Labor Cooperation (NAALC, negotiated by Canada, Mexico and the United States in conjunction with the North American Free Trade Agreement) and the International Labour Organization (ILO). Grievance petitions to these institutions on such matters as freedom of association have significantly raised the international visibility of labour rights problems in Mexico. Although these initiatives are no substitute for more far-reaching reform of Mexico's state-labour relations regime, in some instances international labour-rights campaigns linked to NAALC and ILO proceedings have contributed to progressive change in Mexican government labour policy.

In the Conclusion (Chapter Six), we consider the principal obstacles to democratizing state-labour relations in Mexico and the significant consequences of failing to achieve this transformation. Although the PAN and the PRI have viewed the prospect of federal labour law reform from quite different partisan angles, both parties have had substantial stakes in preserving the institutional status quo. The PAN governments that held power between 2000 and 2012, like their PRI predecessors, found partisan advantage in their alliance with old-line labour leaders. More fundamentally, however, the economic model in place in Mexico since the 1980s relies primarily on tight government controls over wages and strikes, compliant labour organizations and employer-imposed flexibility in the workplace. There is, then, a high degree of compatibility between market-centred economic policies and state-labour practices rooted in the country's authoritarian past. Yet the failure to enact progressive labour law reforms, or to democratize state-labour relations more generally, imposes heavy economic and social costs on both unionized workers and Mexican society as a whole.

Chapter Two
State-Labour Relations in Mexico:
The Legacies of Authoritarian Rule

The core characteristics of state-labour relations in Mexico were defined during the decades immediately following the country's 1910–20 social revolution. Organized labour's entry into national politics proved to be among the most significant consequences of the Mexican Revolution.[1] Although Venustiano Carranza forged a tactical alliance in 1915 with the anarcho-syndicalist House of the World Worker (Casa del Obrero Mundial, COM) that led some seven to ten thousand workers from the Mexico City area — organized as six 'Red Battalions' — to fight with his Constitutionalist forces, the armed peasantry was more important than urban and industrial workers both militarily and politically during the first years of the revolution. However, despite great variations in unions' organizational strength and economic bargaining leverage across different sectors and regions, the labour movement emerged from the protracted revolutionary struggle as the most easily mobilized mass actor in Mexican politics. Because of its significance, revolutionary leaders striving to consolidate their political control and implement the revolution's social and economic agendas were compelled to adopt innovative strategies vis-à-vis organized labour.

These strategies included the adoption of socially progressive labour legislation, the creation of specialized state administrative structures to regulate worker-employer relations and control important aspects of labour participation, and repeated efforts by political and military leaders to establish alliances with leading elements of the organized working class as a way of building popular support and exercising (and centralizing) political power.[2] The inclusion of Article 123 in the new federal constitution (1917) was especially important in this regard. Carranza's delegates to the 1916–17

---

1   This discussion draws on Bensusán, 2000, pp. 101–6, 148 and Middlebrook, 1995, pp. 2, 16–20, 32–3, 45–70, 288–93.

2   For a detailed discussion of the development of state administrative capacity (especially the creation of federal administrative offices and the evolution of tripartite conciliation and arbitration boards) in the labour sector, see Middlebrook, 1995, pp. 45–62.

Constitutional Convention initially backed a proposal that differed little from the reformed 1857 constitution in its simple reaffirmation of liberal guarantees of workers' individual contractual rights. However, under pressure from more radical delegates from states that had already adopted comparatively extensive labour legislation, the Convention eventually voted to include a separate article that guaranteed major collective rights for workers, legitimated expanded state involvement in worker-employer affairs and addressed the main issues on labour's policy agenda. These included: the rights to unionize and to strike; minimum wages and overtime pay; regulations governing working hours, workplace conditions (including occupational health and safety measures) and worker-employer contracts; and the creation of conciliation and arbitration boards to mediate worker-employer conflicts.

The adoption of Article 123 symbolized labour's growing political prominence (it took effect on 1 May 1917).[3] The article established the legal bases for a post-revolutionary state-labour relations regime, marking a turning point regarding the scope of labour legislation and the role played by state administrative institutions responsible for overseeing labour affairs. Legal recognition of unions as bargaining agents in the workplace and constitutional protection of the right to strike were especially important developments in this regard.[4] However, although Article 123 raised social reforms to the level of constitutional guarantees, the Constitutional Convention specifically rejected a proposal for exclusive federal jurisdiction over labour matters. The creation of the Federal Conciliation and Arbitration Board (Junta Federal de Conciliación y Arbitraje, JFCA) in 1927 brought the most strategically important industries under direct federal control, and a constitutional amendment adopted in 1929 granted the federal Congress exclusive authority to legislate on labour matters. Nevertheless, the federal labour law that was eventually adopted in 1931 (and revised in 1970) maintained the distinction between federal and state-level jurisdiction in the resolution of worker-employer conflicts and the overall administration of labour affairs.[5]

---

3   The first official May Day parade held in Mexico City was organized by the COM on 1 May 1913.

4   One measure of the significance of this departure is that the leaders of a general strike in Mexico City in July–August 1916 had been sentenced to death under the terms of an executive order that banned strikes in public services. (The sentence was not carried out.) See Bensusán, 2000, pp. 73–4, for details.

5   See Middlebrook, 1995, table 2.1 for the progressively longer list of industries that came under federal jurisdiction between 1929 and 1990. The federal Ministry of Labour and Social Welfare (Secretaría del Trabajo y Previsión Social, STPS) was established in 1940. Although state-level authorities retain jurisdiction over labour matters in economic activities that are not subject to federal control, they are bound by the provisions of Article 123 and the Federal Labour Law.

Although state-level political authorities consistently opposed attempts to expand the federal government's legal jurisdiction in the labour arena, most worker organizations favoured this development because they considered federal government involvement essential to implement constitutionally mandated reforms at a time when their own overall negotiating weakness in the workplace left in doubt the realization of new social rights.[6] Labour support for state activism was, however, selective. Worker organizations frequently sought government action to force employers to recognize unions, sign collective contracts and improve wages and working conditions, but they opposed state regulation of union formation, internal union activities and strikes.

In the 1931 Federal Labour Law (LFT) and in subsequent legislative reforms, the labour movement won a number of provisions favourable to unions. These included the requirement that an employer sign a collective contract when an officially recognized union solicits one; the recognition of both 'closed shop' provisions in worker-employer contracts[7] and industry-wide collective bargaining agreements (the *contrato-ley*); procedural safeguards for workers' right to strike such as a ban on the hiring of replacement workers while a legally recognised strike is in progress; and the stipulation that employers automatically deduct union dues from workers' paychecks and distribute the proceeds to union officers. The inclusion of union representatives on tripartite conciliation and arbitration boards (composed of labour, business and government representatives) also strengthened organized labour. Furthermore, labour secured legal provisions recognizing a single official bargaining agent in a given workplace, thereby creating a 'closed (or 'union') shop'.

Nevertheless, the labour movement was not strong enough to prevail in some of the key debates that occurred during the 1920s and 1930s concerning the appropriate extent of state authority over labour matters. As a consequence, it was forced to accept administrative controls on various forms of worker

---

6   Although employers strenuously objected to increased state involvement in worker-employer relations following the adoption of Article 123, over time major business organizations also came to support the expansion of federal labour jurisdiction as a way of limiting the radicalism of some state governments. Employers were especially concerned about state laws adopted between 1917 and 1929 regarding worker profit-sharing, given that Article 123 established no parameters in this area and set no limit whatsoever regarding the percentage of profits to be distributed (Bensusán, 2000, pp. 105, 144, 148).

7   Federal labour law recognizes the validity of contracts containing 'entry exclusion clauses' that require workers to join a legally recognized union as a condition of employment, as well as 'separation exclusion clauses' stipulating that an employer must dismiss any worker who loses her or his union membership. These provisions effectively negate Article 123's guarantee that union membership is voluntary. For this reason, the Supreme Court has ruled separation exclusion clauses unconstitutional in three separate decisions issued since 2001. The Court must issue two additional rulings in this same vein before its decisions have general effect in judicial proceedings. See Rendón Corona, 2005, pp. 248n217, 250.

participation.[8] For example, although a group of at least 20 workers has the legal right to form a union without prior authorization, a union cannot negotiate a collective contract with an employer or engage in other activities such as strikes until it is officially registered by either a state-level conciliation and arbitration board or (in the case of unions operating in federal-jurisdiction economic activities) the Ministry of Labour and Social Welfare's (Secretaría del Trabajo y Previsión Social, STPS) Associational Registry (Registro de Asociaciones). Registration procedures are in principle relatively straightforward, but in practice they are subject to purposeful administrative delay and political influence — and unions that cease to meet various legal requirements may lose their registration. Similarly, unions are required to report changes in their leadership and membership within specified time periods, and union officials are not empowered to act until their election is acknowledged by state labour authorities. There is no compulsory arbitration of worker-employer conflicts in Mexico, but federal labour law imposes a number of significant procedural restrictions on strikes.[9] Once established, state controls of this kind proved very difficult to remove.

Many of the most important precedents for these legal restrictions on worker participation were in fact set during the 1920s when the Mexican Regional Labour Confederation (Confederación Regional Obrera Mexicana, CROM) enjoyed a highly favoured position because of its close alliance with post-revolutionary political and military leaders. The CROM, founded in 1918, emerged from the revolutionary struggle as the country's largest labour organization, and during the presidency of Plutarco Elías Calles (1924–8) it came to control part of the state apparatus when its leader, Luis N. Morones, became minister of industry, commerce and labour.[10] In exchange for enforcing

8   Middlebrook, 1995, pp. 62–70. On the origins of mechanisms of control over unions, collective bargaining and strikes, as well as the conflicts among labour, business and government that shaped opportunities for, and restrictions on, the exercise of labour rights, see Bensusán 1992, 2000. See Bensusán, 2007a for a discussion of the practical implications of these various state controls.

9   Since 1938 public-sector employees have been subject to a separate legal regime. For example, the Federal Conciliation and Arbitration Tribunal (Tribunal Federal de Conciliación y Arbitraje, part of the Ministry of the Interior) is responsible for the registration of unions representing public-sector workers. This legislation became the basis for Article 123's 'Section B' in 1960 and the subsequent Federal Law for Public Service Workers (Ley Federal de los Trabajadores al Servicio del Estado) in 1963. In 1996 the Supreme Court ruled that unions representing workers in decentralized agencies of the federal government could re-register under the somewhat less restrictive terms of Article 123's 'Section A.' See Rendón Corona, 2005, pp. 139, 158–9.

10   This discussion draws on Bensusán, 2000, pp. 107, 115–23, 139, 149–50, 195 and Bensusán, 2004, p. 239. Morones was the only nationally prominent labour leader ever to hold such a key cabinet position, although other labour leaders have served as state governors and federal legislators.

stability in worker-employer relations (what CROM leaders described at the time as 'an amnesty in the class struggle') and limiting strikes in those economic activities it dominated, the CROM gained wide latitude to create various institutional mechanisms that helped it expand its membership, confront employers and defeat its rivals in the labour movement.

These arrangements involved, for example, government regulation of the formation of unions and the election of their leaders; the convention of assigning legal control over a collective contract to the union representing the majority (but not necessarily all) of the employees in a particular workplace; the custom of including 'union shop' ('exclusion') clauses in collective contracts, which served as a legal subsidy for unionization without any need to mobilize or retain the support of rank-and-file workers; and legal provisions that concentrate power in the hands of incumbent union leaders and obstruct rank-and-file efforts to hold them accountable. Some of these practices — particularly legal sanction for contract-based exclusion clauses that made union membership obligatory (in contravention of the freedom of association guaranteed by Article 123) and union leaders' authority to seek government sanction of an indefinite strike (binding on all employees in a workplace) without prior consultation with the rank and file or any provision for compulsory arbitration of the dispute — gave labour organizations important coercive powers. In effect, they expanded unions' collective rights at the expense of workers' individual liberties. They were widely criticized by the CROM's labour rivals — and, indeed, by the CROM itself when it was no longer in government — on the grounds that they undermined leadership accountability and union democracy, facilitated the creation of 'ghost unions' and encouraged complicity among government officials, employers and corrupt union leaders.[11] Nonetheless, these arrangements and practices were institutionalized in the 1931 Federal Labour Law, and they were legitimated by the advances that unions won because of their political connections.

The CROM abruptly lost power when its national political alliances collapsed following the assassination of Álvaro Obregón shortly after his re-election as president in 1928, and the Confederation of Mexican Workers

---

Only three of the 21 individuals who headed the Ministry of Labour and Social Welfare between 1940 and 2012 had any significant background in union affairs. Adolfo López Mateos (who headed the STPS between 1952 and 1958 and was president of Mexico between 1958 and 1964), Carlos Gálvez Betancourt (STPS minister in 1975–6) and Francisco Javier Salazar Saénz (STPS minister in 2005–06) all led education workers' unions earlier in their careers. However, none of these individuals was identified politically as a labour leader at the time of his cabinet appointment. See Camp, 2011, p. 1246 and individual biographical entries.

11 In the light of the CROM's practices during the 1920s, it was ironic that CROM delegates to the First Congress on Industrial Relations Law in 1934 argued strongly (albeit unsuccessfully) for legal provisions requiring that all collective contract terms be approved by rank-and-file union members in an open assembly (Bensusán, 2000, p. 226).

(CTM, founded in 1936) eventually replaced it both as the country's largest labour organization and as the most important source of union support for the post-revolutionary regime. Once its political dominance in the labour movement was consolidated in the early 1950s, the CTM became the main recipient of a wide array of state-provided legal, financial and political subsidies (Middlebrook, 1995, pp. 95–105). Government-allied union leaders have, for instance, been the main beneficiaries of federal labour law provisions creating procedural obstacles to challenges by rank-and-file members, as well as the absence of any requirement that union officers be elected by secret ballot.[12] For decades the CTM depended on government financial support — apparently channelled to it through Mexico's long-ruling 'official' party, the Institutional Revolutionary Party (PRI) — because it was incapable of collecting sufficient membership dues to fund its operations. As the PRI's official labour sector, the CTM also occasionally benefited from the government's use of force against its union rivals, and it relied on the PRI's overwhelming dominance in the electoral arena to place its candidates in elective office, through which its affiliates enjoyed opportunities for both upward political mobility and (often illicit) material gains.[13]

More generally, the CTM and other government-allied unions benefited disproportionately from some publicly financed social welfare programmes, including subsidized access to basic commodities, housing and consumer credit. Indeed, the CTM virtually monopolized labour representation on tripartite conciliation and arbitration boards and on the governing bodies of institutions like the Mexican Social Security Institute (Instituto Mexicano del Seguro Social, IMSS), the National Minimum Wage Commission (Comisión Nacional de los Salarios Mínimos, CNSM) and the National Commission for Worker Profit-Sharing (Comisión Nacional para la Participación de los Trabajadores en las Utilidades). For many years it also claimed the lion's share of the benefits provided by the National Worker Housing Institute (Instituto del Fondo Nacional de la Vivienda para los Trabajadores) and the Workers'

12 Union statutes requiring that elections be held in an open general assembly (thereby exposing political dissidents), or those that erect obstacles to rank-and-file challenges, have the force of law once they are approved by STPS authorities or local (state-level) conciliation and arbitration boards. Similarly, whereas federal labour law permits one-third of a union's members to convene a general assembly if, ten days following their request the union's leadership fails to do so, the legal quorum is two-thirds of the union's total membership. This higher quorum requirement (it is normally 51 per cent of the union's membership) is a significant obstacle to the mobilization of internal opposition against an entrenched union leadership (Middlebrook, 1995, p. 67).

13 One constraint on the CTM's influence within the PRI was that public-sector employees were organized by the Federation of Public Service Workers' Unions (Federación de Sindicatos de Trabajadores al Servicio del Estado, formed in 1938), which was affiliated with the party's 'popular' sector.

Bank (Banco Obrero, BO). In many instances, these were benefits that labour organizations would have had difficulty winning on their own; securing them depended mainly on their alliance with political elites. In return, the CTM and similar organizations offered reliable backing for post-revolutionary governments, support that was particularly valuable during periods of economic or political crisis.

This was, however, a highly unequal alliance. Linking the CTM to the 'official' party symbolized organized labour's inclusion in Mexico's post-revolutionary governing coalition. However, legal restrictions on union formation, internal union activities and strikes — backed by the governing elite's effective control over the means of coercion and state officials' willingness to use force when necessary to achieve their objectives — established the de jure and de facto parameters of labour action. Unions' dependence on state subsidies, and union leaders' consequent greater reliance on political alliances than on the mobilization of rank-and-file support, made them vulnerable to government pressure. Indeed, the ability of 'official' labour organizations to preserve their preferential access to public resources depended primarily on their willingness to control the actions of rank-and-file union members. This dependence was often accentuated by the labour movement's own weaknesses, including its heterogeneous organizational composition, the comparatively small size of many unions and the frequent absence of effective representational arrangements linking labour leaders with rank-and-file members.

Over time, the contradictory terms of the 'official' labour movement's relationship with the ruling elite turned government-allied unions into important mechanisms of political control. Their efforts to block working-class mobilization, limit organizational pluralism in the labour sector and restrain workers' demands, combined with restrictive legal provisions and state administrative practices, constituted central elements of political authoritarianism in Mexico. At the same time, the preservation of a governing coalition in which organized labour was a major partner infused Mexico's post-revolutionary regime with remarkable resilience, permitting it to surmount diverse political and economic pressures for change. And even after the electoral defeat of the 'official' party in the 2000 presidential election, the survival of the state-labour relations regime established in the 1920s and 1930s and the residual influence of labour organizations like the CTM continued to shape government-labour relations in significant ways.

Chapter Three
Organized Labour Under Pressure:
The Impacts of Economic Restructuring and
Political Democratization

During the 1980s and 1990s, Mexico experienced dual economic and political transitions. For much of this period, however, the liberalization of Mexico's authoritarian regime proceeded much more slowly than economic restructuring. Indeed, the core characteristics of Mexican authoritarianism — the concentrated power of the federal executive, economic policymakers' general insulation from socio-political opposition and long-established state controls over mass actors like organized labour — contributed substantially to the speed and relative ease with which far-reaching market-liberalizing reforms were enacted from the mid-1980s through the early 1990s. The fact that economic opening occurred while many elements of authoritarian rule remained intact also meant that worker organizations and other popular groups had limited capacity to redress their needs or influence national policy debates so as to define a more socially inclusive economic strategy. This is one important reason why, although electoral democratization has altered the political opportunities available to workers and unions, economic restructuring has had far more significant consequences for the Mexican labour movement.

Economic Restructuring and its Consequences for Labour

From the 1940s through the 1970s, the alliance between Mexico's governing political elite and the 'official' labour movement centred on an import-substitution model of economic development whose goal was to supply national demand with domestically manufactured consumer durable goods and intermediate products rather than with foreign imports.[1] Mexican policymakers' ability to deliver steady economic expansion (Mexico's gross domestic product [GDP] rose by an average of 6.2 per cent per year in inflation-adjusted terms between 1940 and 1970, and by 6.4 per cent per year between 1951 and 1980) and rising per capita income (per capita GDP grew by 2.9 per cent per year

---

1   This discussion draws on Middlebrook, 1995, pp. 209–22.

in real terms between 1940 and 1970 and by 3.3 per cent per year between 1951 and 1980)[2] while at the same time restraining inflation, especially during the 'stabilizing development' period from the late 1950s through the 1960s, depended to a significant degree on effective political control over organized workers. The combination of legal and administrative constraints on different forms of labour participation (especially collective bargaining and strikes) and reliable support from the Confederation of Mexican Workers (CTM) and other 'official' labour organizations gave government officials a substantial degree of decision-making autonomy in economic matters.

At the same time, sustained economic growth and the characteristics of import-substituting industrialization reinforced the governing political elite's pact with labour. Rapid industrial expansion generated new sources of employment and opportunities for social mobility, and particularly after the mid-1950s rising real wages and expanding social welfare benefits substantially improved many workers' standard of living.[3] Because high tariff barriers and direct import controls protected domestic producers from foreign competition, many private-sector firms could maintain comfortable profit margins despite rising wages.[4] Indeed, as workers' incomes and consumption capacity rose, producers benefited from an expanding domestic market. As a result, despite the fact that over the longer term import-substitution policies created a number of problems that contributed to serious economic difficulties during the 1970s and 1980s, the interests of both labour and domestic capital converged around them. In turn, the ability of labour leaders to deliver substantial resources to their members — in the form of both rising wages and expanding access to government-subsidized housing, health care, financial credit, retirement funds and so forth — strengthened their position within government-allied unions.

This convergence of interests between labour and domestic capital was, however, seriously challenged by the financial crisis that struck Mexico in August 1982.[5] In the years following the government's sudden suspension of payments on its external debt, economic growth collapsed and inflation

2   The data for the 1940–70 period are from Moreno-Brid and Ros, 2009, table A.1; the data for the 1951–80 period are from Urquidi, 2003, table 15.1.

3   Although the inflation-adjusted value of the daily minimum wage in Mexico City declined from 1938 (index value = 100) through 1951 (44.4), from the mid-1950s it rose quite consistently to its peak in 1976 (158.8) (Middlebrook, 1995, table 6.1). Similarly, the coverage of government health and welfare programmes, especially those directed toward unionized employees in the formal sector, expanded substantially from the 1940s to the 1970s (Zapata, 1986, pp. 126–7). Real wage increases were based on steadily rising labour productivity (Hernández Laos, 2006, table 1).

4   A fixed exchange rate between 1954 and 1976 also stabilized the environment for worker-employer negotiations by insulating the economy from external shocks.

5   See Lustig, 1992 for a discussion of the origins of the 1982 debt crisis and its economic impact.

spiralled to record levels.[6] The administration of President Miguel de la Madrid (1982–8) was compelled to adopt austerity measures (including stringent limits on wage increases, cuts in government social spending, price increases on many basic commodities and reduced government subsidies for mass transportation, electricity, natural gas and gasoline) that severely eroded workers' incomes and standards of living.[7] Heterodox economic policies — including a tripartite Economic Solidarity Pact (Pacto de Solidaridad Económica) that the government negotiated with labour and business in December 1987 — eventually brought inflation under control. However, the inflation-adjusted value of the daily minimum wage in Mexico City fell by 49.7 per cent between 1982 and 1988 (with the sharpest fall in 1983),[8] and unemployment in some sectors and regions remained high throughout the 1980s because of economic retrenchment in the private sector and the government's decision to close unprofitable state-owned enterprises. The wage share of national income declined from 43.2 per cent in 1982 to 34.6 per cent in 1987 (Álvarez Béjar, 1991, table 2.1).[9]

More generally, Presidents De la Madrid and Carlos Salinas de Gortari (1988–94) responded to the debt crisis and the apparent 'exhaustion' of import-substituting industrialization by embracing a new economic model that featured trade and exchange-rate liberalization, the deregulation of foreign investment flows and financial markets, the abandonment of sector-specific industrial and employment-promotion policies and the aggressive privatization of state-owned enterprises.[10] This package of market-liberalizing reforms did

6   The inflation-adjusted rate of GDP growth, which had averaged 5.5 per cent per year from 1970 to 1977 and 8.4 per cent per year from 1978 to 1981 during a petroleum-led economic boom, fell to an average of -0.1 per cent from 1982 to 1988. Consumer price inflation averaged 88 per cent per year between 1982 and 1988 and reached an annual rate of 177 per cent in January 1988 (Middlebrook, 1995, pp. 257–9).

7   For an assessment of the economic challenges that organized labour faced during the 1980s and the labour movement's responses, see Middlebrook, 1995, pp. 255–69. Boltvinik, 2003 (especially pp. 415–8) provides a detailed analysis of the evolution of government social expenditure during the 1980s and its impact on poverty and inequality.

8   Authors' calculation based on data presented in Middlebrook, 1995, table 6.1. Other measures of wages and income showed a similar pattern of decline. The minimum wage in Mexico fell by 42.4 per cent over the 1982–8 period, while average contractual wages and average manufacturing income declined by 38.1 per cent and 33.5 per cent, respectively (Burgess, 2004, table 3.2). See also Dávila Capalleja, 1997.

9   The wage share of national income fell even more in the early 1990s, reaching 27.9 per cent in 1992 (El Día, 10 Dec. 1992, p. 1).

10   The total number of state-owned firms, decentralized agencies and investment trusts fell from 1,555 in 1982 to 232 in 1992. The wave of privatizations included some of Mexico's largest state-owned firms, including the two airline companies, the two largest copper-mining companies, the largest telecommunications firm, steel mills and the commercial banks, which had been nationalized at the onset of the debt crisis in 1982 (Valdés Ugalde, 1994, tables 9.2, 9.3 and figure 9.1).

     For an overview of these policies and an analysis of the political factors that explain the

succeed in attracting substantial new flows of foreign investment (especially after the North American Free Trade Agreement [NAFTA] among Canada, Mexico and the United States took effect in January 1994), and it stimulated a dramatic expansion in manufactured exports. However, a very significant share of these goods was produced in low-wage processing (*maquiladora*) plants that had only weak productive linkages to the rest of the economy. Nor did Mexico's new economic model generate sufficient formal-sector employment to absorb an expanding labour supply, or recoup the high average economic growth rates that had been achieved under import-substitution policies. Indeed, despite short periods of relatively rapid economic expansion in 1989–92 and 1996–2000, the inflation-adjusted rate of GDP growth averaged just 2.4 per cent per year for the entire 1981–2000 period. The annual per capita rate of GDP growth averaged only 0.4 per cent in real terms over this period (Urquidi, 2003, table 15.1).

Radical economic restructuring posed serious challenges for government-allied and more politically independent unions alike.[11] The widespread closure or privatization of state-owned enterprises undercut what had long been the principal advantage of some of Mexico's largest and most influential labour organizations: their ability to use their political influence to win concessions from state managers in negotiations over wages, benefit levels and working conditions. Indeed, in preparing state-owned enterprises for sale to private investors, the government often forced upon workers deep cuts in staffing, wages and fringe benefits, as well as sharply altered contract terms that significantly expanded management prerogatives and limited unions' influence in enterprise affairs.[12] More generally, the shift in the balance of power between the public and private sectors that occurred after the mid-1980s substantially reduced organized labour's overall political leverage even though the Institutional Revolutionary Party (PRI) still retained control over the federal government.

A similar restructuring process unfolded in private-sector firms, often with active government support — and, in some notable instances, the use of public force. In many industries, firms slashed employment, cut wages and benefits and attempted to raise productivity by revising contract terms and redefining work rules. More generally, they stiffened their opposition to union influence

extent and speed of economic restructuring, see Middlebrook and Zepeda, 2003, pp. 6–16 and Bensusán and Cook, 2003. Bensusán (2000, table 6.1) summarizes the principal phases of the economic restructuring process.

11 Employment in the manufacturing sector as a whole fell by 11.8 per cent between 1980 and 1989, while employment declined even more sharply (by 48 per cent between 1981 and 1990) in public-sector manufacturing firms (Middlebrook, 1995, p. 258).

12 See Middlebrook, 1995, p. 256; De la Garza, 1998; Williams, 2001; McLeod, 2004, pp. 134–40, 164–6, 184, 216–8, 225, 228; Zapata, 2006, pp. 2, 7–8.

in production processes and to unionization itself.[13] Industry-wide collective bargaining agreements (*contratos-ley*), which established uniform wages and working conditions in the textile, sugar, rubber and radio and television industries, were a particular target of business and government opposition. Companies also increasingly adopted subcontracting arrangements via non-unionized subsidiaries that undermined unions' role (Esquinca and Melgoza Valdivia, 2006, pp. 462–3).

At the same time, employer groups lobbied persistently for changes in the Federal Labour Law (LFT) that would enhance flexibility in hiring and working practices and further limit the right to strike. However, in contrast to what occurred in some Latin American countries that adopted market-liberalizing reforms during the 1980s and 1990s (Madrid, 2003, p. 54), Mexico's economic opening was not anchored in formal changes in labour law. The CTM, whose organizational presence, membership and overall influence depended much more on legal subsidies than on sectoral bargaining strength or mobilized rank-and-file support, saw labour law reform as a substantial threat and manoeuvred to block it.[14]

In the period between Salinas de Gortari's designation as the PRI's candidate in October 1987 and his accession to the presidency in December 1988, the CTM itself had initiated discussions about labour law reform. At the outset of the Salinas administration the Ministry of Labour and Social Welfare (STPS) established a tripartite commission to begin analysis of the matter, and in August 1989 the federal Chamber of Deputies held formal hearings to elicit testimony from experts in the field. However, a combination of factors — the Salinas administration's demonstrated intention to curtail many established labour prerogatives, the fact that business interests wielded considerable political influence in the Salinas government, the expanded presence of leftist critics of the 'official' labour movement in the Chamber of Deputies following the sharply contested 1988 elections, and the labour movement's own weakened bargaining position — all made the CTM fear that it might have little say over the final content of revised national labour legislation. The CTM and other labour organizations could not prevent the Salinas administration from interpreting and applying existing legal provisions so as to provide employers with the flexibility to redraw collective contracts, redefine workplace industrial relations and adopt in practice the various changes they sought to incorporate into law. Nevertheless, perhaps in part because negotiations over the NAFTA

13 Middlebrook, 1995, p. 256; Bensusán, 2004, pp. 251–2; Bensusán, 2007a, p. 20.

14 This discussion draws on Middlebrook, 1995, p. 298, and Bensusán, 2000, pp. 410–11. On the numerous proposals for labour law reform from the late 1980s onward, see Bensusán, 2000, pp. 395–454; Bensusán, 2003, pp. 55–93; Bizberg, 2003, pp. 235–8; Zapata, 2006.

(the Salinas administration's top policy priority, and an initiative that the CTM supported) made labour rights in Mexico a highly sensitive political issue, the CTM successfully exerted pressure on the government not to proceed with labour law reform. Under these circumstances, the STPS suspended formal discussions of the topic in January 1992.[15]

Although neither the Salinas government nor the administration of Ernesto Zedillo Ponce de León (1994–2000) managed to implement formal changes in labour law, employers proceeded — often with the tacit or active support of federal and state-level labour officials — to adopt a range of informal strategies designed to achieve their goal of radically flexibilizing industrial relations. In particular, 'ghost unions' (unions whose existence may be unknown to rank-and-file members, but which are legally registered with employer support as a means of avoiding the formation of more accountable worker organizations) and 'employer protection contracts' (agreements negotiated between an employer and an unaccountable or spurious union leadership, whose main purpose is to defend management prerogatives in the workplace) proliferated after the 1980s and became major obstacles to grassroots union organizing (Bensusán, 2007a, pp. 20–1, 24–5, *passim*).[16]

15 Following the suspension of negotiations over labour law reform, the Salinas administration pursued a parallel path to legitimate the changes that were taking place in labour relations practices. In May 1992 the government and leading labour and employer organizations signed the National Accord for the Elevation of Productivity and Quality (Acuerdo Nacional para la Elevación de la Productividad y la Calidad), the provisions of which became the main principles in the 1995 agreement to promote a 'new labour culture' (Bensusán, 2000, pp. 411–24; 2003, p. 59).

Although the CTM and other Labour Congress (CT) affiliates managed to block significant labour law reform during the late 1980s and 1990s, they were compelled to accept important changes in social welfare policy. The 'official' labour movement initially rejected outright the Salinas administration's proposal to replace the 'pay-as-you-go', defined-benefit public pension system with a defined-contribution private system (featuring mandatory individual retirement accounts) modelled on the privatized system adopted by Chile in 1980–1. However, whereas informal labour-flexibilization strategies sufficed in lieu of a major reform of the Federal Labour Law, the growing financial difficulties facing the Mexican Social Security Institute (IMSS) and the Social Security Institute for State Workers (Instituto de Seguridad y Servicios Sociales de los Trabajadores del Estado, ISSSTE) required constitutional and legal reforms. In part by underscoring the political costs it ostensibly incurred by not acting on employer demands for LFT reform, the Salinas administration successfully pressured the Labour Congress into accepting the creation of the Retirement Saving System (Sistema de Ahorro para el Retiro, SAR) in 1992 as a supplement to the IMSS and ISSSTE pension systems. The measure was ostensibly designed to relieve financial pressures on the IMSS and to increase national savings. In practice, however, its most signficant consequences were to strengthen the banks and other private financial firms that managed individual retirement accounts and to open the way for more extensive privatizing reforms of the IMSS in 1995 and 2004, as well as of the ISSSTE in 2007. For an overview of changes in the retirement-pension system, see Bertranou, 1995; Espinosa-Vega and Sinha, 2000; Laurell, 2003; Madrid, 2003, pp. 83–6; Dion, 2010, pp. 121–2, 171–87.

16 A 1980 revision to the Federal Labour Law (article 923) that permitted conciliation and arbitration boards to reject strike petitions demanding the negotiation of a new collective

It is notable that, in marked contrast to the 'state withdrawal' agenda that economic reformers pursued in other arenas, government officials during the 1980s and 1990s showed little interest in dismantling the complex array of legal and administrative controls regulating union formation, wage and contract negotiations and strikes.[17] In fact, limiting wage increases in order to control inflation and make low levels of worker compensation a basis of international comparative advantage became a key element in government economic strategy. As part of their efforts to contain wage increases and break the established link between legal minimum wages and 'market-determined' wages, the De la Madrid and Salinas administrations used their executive powers to hold minimum wages in line with restrictive macroeconomic targets. Indeed, they departed from long-established practice by employing the percentage increase in the official minimum wage not as a reference point for contract negotiations conducted by individual unions and private firms, but as a limit on annual wage increases.[18] Because minimum-wage trends influence adjustments in many labour contracts (Fairris, Popli and Zepeda, 2001), overall wage levels therefore remained depressed.

As a result, despite some periods of economic growth and steady gains in labour productivity (especially in the manufacturing sector), the real (inflation-adjusted) value of the minimum wage fell by a cumulative 70.2 per cent between 1981 and 1997, and wages stagnated from the late 1990s through 2009.[19] The data reported in Table 1 show that minimum wages fell sharply in the wake of the devastating 1994–5 financial crisis, stabilized at a significantly lower level between 1996 and 1998, and then slowly eroded through much of the period until 2009 — reaching a level in 2009 that was 28 per cent lower than in 1994. The 2008 level was approximately 20 per cent below Mexico's

contract in workplaces where an agreement is already registered had the effect of increasing employers' incentives to secure protection contracts (Bensusán, 2007a, p. 8, *passim*).

    Some analysts estimate that as many as 90 per cent of the collective agreements registered by state-level conciliation and arbitration boards are in fact protection contracts. See Bensusán, 2007a, pp. 20–1, 24–5; Bouzas Ortiz and Reyes Ramos, 2007.

17 This discussion follows Middlebrook and Zepeda, 2003, p. 15.

18 See Dávila Capalleja, 1997, pp. 304–5 for a discussion of the declining effectiveness of the minimum wage between 1976 and 1987.

19 Bensusán, 2000, table 6.3. See Bensusán, 2000, figure 6.1 and Hernández Laos, 2006, tables 1, 2 on labour productivity trends. Mexico was one of the few countries (the others included Bolivia, the Dominican Republic, Guatemala and Honduras) in Latin America that registered a decline in real minimum wage levels over the 1995–2007 period. Argentina, Brazil, Chile and Uruguay all saw substantial minimum wage gains during these years, and in all of these countries the minimum wage significantly exceeded the poverty line. Similarly, whereas minimum wages as a proportion of average wages increased in Argentina, Brazil, Chile and Uruguay between 1995–7 and 2004–05, this ratio declined in Mexico (International Labour Organization [ILO], 2008a).

Table 1. Inflation-Adjusted Wages and Income in Mexico, 1994–2009

Year	Average Daily Minimum Wage		Average Monthly Income of Salaried Workers
	Pesos	Index value	Pesos
1994	13.98	100.0	NA
1995	12.08	86.5	3,514
1996	10.89	77.9	2,985
1997	10.82	77.4	2,954
1998	10.90	78.0	3,042
1999	10.51	75.2	3,004
2000	10.60	75.8	3,378
2001	10.65	76.2	3,556
2002	10.72	76.7	3,624
2003	10.65	76.2	3,699
2004	10.50	75.1	3,733
2005	10.50	75.1	3,711
2006	10.48	75.0	3,825
2007	10.42	74.5	3,925
2008	10.20	73.0	3,821
2009	10.06	72.0	3,671

Source: Bensusán and Middlebrook, 2012, table 15.1. Minimum daily wage data (expressed in constant 1994 pesos) are from Secretaría del Trabajo y Previsión Social-Comisión Nacional de los Salarios Mínimos, 2010. Average monthly income data for salaried workers (14 years and older, expressed in constant 2002 pesos) are from Salas, 2010.

NA = not available

official poverty line. In 2008 some 38 per cent of Mexico's salaried labour force earned no more than two minimum wages.[20]

Similarly, the inflation-adjusted average monthly income of salaried workers age 14 years and older rose by only 4.5 per cent over the entire 1995–2009 period (an average annual increase of merely 0.3 per cent; see Table 1). As with the minimum wage, real monthly income also fell significantly following the 1994–5 crisis and only recovered its 1995 level in 2001. It reached its peak of 3,925 (constant 2002) pesos in 2007, before declining again in 2008–9 as

20   ILO, 2008a; Banco de México, 2009. In March 2010, the share of the working population earning less than three minimum wages (an amount up to 172 pesos per day, equivalent to about US$13 at the prevailing exchange rate) reached 58 per cent, representing a total of 25.5 million workers (González, 2010).

an international financial crisis once more pushed the Mexican economy into recession.[21]

One of the reasons successive presidential administrations were able to impose such restrictive wage policies over a sustained period, at the same time that the number of strikes declined sharply (see below), was that many workers lacked authentic union representation committed to improving their economic welfare. This situation produced highly negative consequences both for millions of working-class families and for Mexico's capacity to develop an internal consumers' market capable of supporting firm-level technological and organizational innovation.

The cumulative impacts of far-reaching economic restructuring and major changes in government labour policy were also evident in three other areas: a notable decline in the unionization rate and a shift in the sociological profile of the unionized labour force; labour unions' diminished capacity to mobilize in defence of their interests; and growing organizational fragmentation of the labour movement.[22]

Unionization

Data concerning the size of Mexico's unionized labour force and the unionization rate (that is, the proportion of the workforce that is unionized) in different economic sectors and geographic areas are notoriously inconsistent and often unreliable.[23] Nevertheless, the available sources all concur that the unionized share of the economically active population (EAP) declined significantly between the late 1970s and the early 1990s. In 1978, some 16.3 per cent of the EAP aged 14 years (the minimum legal working age) and older were unionized, but by 1994 this proportion had fallen to 10.4 per cent (see Table 2).[24] It is difficult to judge the reliability of National Institute

21 Declining employment in large manufacturing plants as a proportion of total manufacturing employment meant that workers also lost access to the important fringe benefits that jobs in large firms typically provide (Middlebrook and Zepeda, 2003, pp. 30–1).

22 This discussion follows Bensusán and Middlebrook, 2012, pp. 342–6.

23 The STPS's Associational Registry (for federal-jurisdiction economic activities) and state-level conciliation and arbitration boards (for state-jurisdiction economic activities) compile data on union membership. However, these numbers are considered unreliable because they are based largely on reports filed by unions (whose leaders have a political incentive to inflate membership totals), which may be incomplete, inaccurate or out of date. Most analysts rely, therefore, on the National Survey of Household Income and Expenditure conducted in 1984, 1989 and then every two years since 1992 by the National Institute for Statistics, Geography and Informatics (INEGI), although these surveys also have some methodological limitations. The data reported in Table 2 are drawn from the INEGI surveys. For a discussion of the difficulties posed by different measures of unionization in Mexico, see de la Garza, 2006a.

24 The figure for 1978 is from Zazueta and de la Peña, 1984, table II.11. The data on union membership employed by Zazueta and de la Peña came from the STPS's Associational Registry and state-level conciliation and arbitration boards. Using these same sources, Aguilar García (2001, p. 386) calculated that the unionized share of the EAP declined to 10.9 per cent in 2000.

Table 2. Union Membership and Unionization Rates in Mexico, 1992–2006

	1992	1994	2000	2002	2006
Economically active population (EAP)	30,261,606	35,037,931	41,026,994	41,983,675	44,709,819
Industrial labour force	8,119,017	8,694,003	10,085,329	12,542,175	NA
Industrial labour force subject to unionization (ILFSU)	6,523,233	6,761,930	8,028,614	9,661,375	NA
Union members	4,116,920	3,632,267	4,025,878	4,199,320	4,343,920
Men	2,730,809	2,191,897	2,320,830	2,461,890	2,494,000*
Women	1,386,111	1,440,370	1,705,048	1,737,430	1,849,000*
Union members in ILFSU	1,443,995	1,007,128	1,208,164	1,453,460	NA
Men	1,212,473	817,923	916,165	1,120,550	
Women	231,522	189,205	291,999	332,910	
Unionized share of EAP (per cent)	13.6	10.4	9.8	10.0	9.7
Unionized share of ILFSU (per cent)	22.2	14.9	15.0	15.0	NA

NA = Not available   * Data rounded to nearest thousand in original source

Sources: Bensusán and Middlebrook, 2012, table 15.2 (data for 1992, 2000 and 2002, Esquinca and Melgosa Valdivia, 2006, table 1; for 1994, Herrera and Melgosa, 2003, table XIV.1; for 2006, Zepeda, 2011, p. 249, figure 6.1, table 6.5).

Note: The 'industrial labour force subject to unionization' consists of blue-collar salaried workers, 14 years and older, employed in industrial establishments.

for Statistics, Geography and Informatics (Instituto Nacional de Estadística, Geografía e Informática, INEGI) survey data showing a sharp fall in the total number of union members between 1992 and 1994 (Table 2), before the onset of Mexico's severe 1994–5 economic crisis and during a period when the size of both the industrial labour force and the EAP continued to expand. However, data for the 1994–2006 period consistently show that about one-tenth of the EAP was unionized.[25] The unionized share of the industrial labour force subject to unionization — a subset of the EAP that excludes, for example, the very large and difficult-to-organize informal sector — was consistently bigger (about 15 per cent), but the available data show a similarly substantial drop between 1992 and 2006 (Table 2).[26]

Although the unionization rate in some economic sectors oscillated over this period, the overall trend was a broad secular decline.[27] Those industries (mining and petroleum extraction, for example) and occupations (education workers, for instance) that were most heavily unionized in the mid-1980s remained so in the late 1990s (Fairris and Levine, 2004, pp. 11–4). A similar trend held for the geographic distribution of the unionized population; the Federal District and the states of México and Nuevo León had the highest concentrations of union members at both the beginning and the end of this period (Esquinca and Melgoza Valdivia, 2006, table 4; Zepeda, 2011, p. 254). There were, however, some important changes in the sociological characteristics of the unionized population. The average age of the unionized labour force increased somewhat

25 Using data from the STPS's Associational Registry and state-level conciliation and arbitration boards, Zepeda (2011, figure 6.1) calculated that 11.4 per cent of the EAP was unionized in 2006.

Fairris and Levine (2004, pp. 10–11, 16), who restricted the sample population in various ways, concluded that union density declined from 30.3 per cent in 1984 to 20.8 per cent in 1998. Fairris (2006, figure 1) concurred that the largest declines in union density occurred between 1984 and 1989 and between 1992 and 1994. De la Garza (2012) presents evidence suggesting that there may have been a further general decline in union density following the 2008–09 international financial crisis, which led to widespread plant closings in Mexico.

26 Over the 2005–09 period, an average of 27.5 per cent of the EAP worked in the informal sector (defined as household-based economic activities not formally registered as enterprises). See INEGI, 2010.

27 In examining the causes of this decline, Fairris and Levine (2004, pp. 14–6) assessed the impact of both compositional factors ('changes in the industrial, occupational, or geographical composition of jobs in the economy, or ... changes in the education, age, and gender composition of workers in the labor force') and institutional changes ('changing support for unions by government actors or a changing desire for, or resistance to, unions by workers or employers'), although they noted that these elements were not necessarily independent of one another. For example, one change that contributed to a national-level decline in union density was the growing relative importance of employment in the *maquiladora* sector concentrated in states along Mexico's northern border, where union density has historically been low. However, because union density declined in nearly every industrial, occupational, demographic and geographical category, Fairris and Levine concluded that the shift was due principally to 'the overall institutional climate for organizing and retaining union members' (2004, p. 14).

between 1992 and 2002 as the unionization rate among younger cohorts fell, and the average educational attainment of unionized workers rose over time (Esquinca and Melgoza Valdivia, 2006, tables 2, 3). Indeed, graduates (those with more than a university education) were the demographic category showing the greatest increase in union density between 1984 and 1998 (Fairris and Levine, 2004, table 2). The aggregate number of unionized male workers actually shrank over the 1992–2006 period (Table 2), and the proportion of women among all union members increased quite consistently over time, from 33.7 per cent in 1992 to 42.6 per cent in 2006.[28]

The declining unionization rate had palpable consequences for workers. In the late 1990s unionized employees still received higher wages and fringe benefits (both in terms of the amount received by each worker and fringe benefits as a proportion of total compensation), and they secured more employer-provided occupational training, than did their non-unionized counterparts. This 'union premium' had, however, declined over time. Whereas in 1984 unions bid up wages by some 21 per cent, by 1996 this premium had declined to 15 per cent. Similarly, whereas in 1992 unionized establishments in the manufacturing sector offered 143 per cent more fringe benefits per worker (including such items as private health care and pension benefits, transportation costs, educational expenses for workers' dependent children, a Christmas bonus, child care and subsidized loans) than non-union establishments, the advantage in 1999 was only 26 per cent (Fairris, 2006, pp. 16–21).[29] It was higher for women than for men (Esquinca and Melgoza Valdivia, 2006, p. 480).

A decline in the union premium meant that individual workers had fewer material incentives to join unions. Of course, unionization in Mexico is rarely voluntary. Employers, government officials and corrupt or unaccountable labour leaders may collude to register a trade union without the prior consent of rank-and-file employees in a particular workplace (indeed, even before workers are hired or a plant begins operations), and the existence of a 'ghost union' may be entirely unknown to its ostensible members. Yet as the federal government responded to the incentive of multiparty electoral competition by gradually extending public welfare to the general population through such programmes as Opportunities (Oportunidades, a social assistance programme that provides conditional cash transfers to poor families) and Popular Insurance (Seguro Popular, a government-subsidized, voluntary health insurance programme), individuals — even those employed in Mexico's very large informal sector — found it progressively easier to gain access to welfare benefits that previously had in practice been restricted to salaried workers in

28 Authors' calculations based on data presented in Table 2.

29 These differences were statistically significant at the 0.01 level. Fairris (2006, pp. 16–7) also presents data showing that unions reduced wage inequality in Mexico, although this effect also grew weaker over the 1984–96 period.

the formal sector of the economy. In this context, institutional arrangements like the 'entry exclusion clause' (a provision typically included in a collective work agreement requiring that an individual join the legally recognized union as a condition of employment) assumed even greater importance as a legal support for the organized labour movement.[30]

Labour Mobilization

The incidence of labour strikes also declined notably after the mid-1990s. A lower level of unionization and unions' reduced capacity to mobilize in defence of workers' interests probably contributed to this trend, but part of the explanation no doubt lies in government officials' use of legal controls to block labour mobilization.[31] Previous research has shown that government officials have historically maintained tighter controls on strikes in more strategically important federal-jurisdiction industries than in heterogeneous, less politically sensitive state-jurisdiction economic activities. Indeed, an analysis of official data for the period between 1941 and 1993 found that, although there was a weak but statistically significant relationship between changes in the volume of federal-jurisdiction strike petitions and fluctuations in the annual rate of inflation, there was no significant relationship between variations in the

30 In debates after 2001 concerning possible modifications to the Federal Labour Law, all the parties responsible for submitting reform bills to the Congress responded to the Supreme Court's rulings against separation exclusion clauses in contracts by eliminating them. Yet even the National Union of Workers (Unión Nacional de Trabajadores, UNT), the national confederation most committed to democratizing state-labour relations, argued that it was necessary to preserve the entry exclusion clause in order to ensure the survival of the organized labour movement. It also argued for maintaining employers' legal obligation to deduct union dues from workers' paychecks and transfer them to union authorities. See, for example, the legislative proposals made by the Party of the Democratic Revolution (Partido de la Revolución Democrática, PRD) in Cámara de Diputados, *Gaceta Parlamentaria*, nos. 2882-IV and 2992-III (20 Apr. 2010).

31 Of course, because the widespread presence of exclusion clauses in collective contracts makes union membership a condition of employment rather than a voluntary commitment to a truly representative organization, and because the organizational successes of many traditional unions are often mainly the product of government support, the unionization rate cannot necessarily be taken as a reliable indicator of unions' economic and political power or as a measure of their capacity (or willingness) to mobilize against public policies they oppose (Bensusán, 2004, p. 272).

The Federal Labour Law limits legal (*existente*) strikes to the suspension of work to achieve specified goals. The strike must be supported by the majority of workers employed in a given company or work centre, and workers must present to the employer and the appropriate conciliation and arbitration board six days (ten days in the case of public service employees) before suspending work a formal petition (*emplazamiento*) that specifies the goals and time of the strike action. For this reason, the renegotiation of collective contracts and industry-wide collective bargaining agreements (once per year on salary issues and every two years on workplace conditions and general contract terms) generally includes the filing of a strike petition, even though only a very small proportion of these petitions actually leads to a legal strike. For further details, see Middlebrook, 1995, p. 69.

Table 3. Labour Strike Petitions and Strikes in Federal-Jurisdiction Industries in Mexico, 1989–2010

Year	Strike Petitions	Strikes	Ratio of Strikes to Petitions
1989	6,806	118	0.017
1990	6,395	150	0.023
1991	7,006	136	0.019
1992	6,814	156	0.023
1993	7,531	155	0.020
1994	7,573	116	0.015
[1989–94 annual average]	7,021	138	0.020
1995	7,676	96	0.012
1996	7,621	51	0.007
1997	8,047	39	0.005
1998	7,352	33	0.004
1999	7,972	32	0.004
2000	8,282	26	0.003
[1995–2000 annual average]	7,825	46	0.006
2001	6,821	35	0.005
2002	6,042	45	0.007
2003	5,909	44	0.007
2004	6,122	38	0.006
2005	6,646	50	0.007
2006	7,390	55	0.007
[2001–06 annual average]	6,488	44	0.007
2007	9,045	28	0.003
2008	10,814	21	0.002
2009	13,207	19	0.001
2010	12,682	11	0.001
[2007–10 annual average]	11,437	20	0.002

Source: Bensusán and Middlebrook, 2012, table 15.3 (Dirección General de Investigación y Estadísticas del Trabajo, Secretaría del Trabajo y Previsión Social (www.stps.gob.mx)). The data for 2010 are preliminary. Both period averages and the ratio of strikes to petitions are the authors' calculations. The period averages are rounded numbers.

number of strikes and shifting economic conditions. Nor was there a consistent relationship between the overall character of presidential labour policy (that is, whether it was liberal or conservative) and the number of legally recognized strikes in federal industries.[32]

Trends concerning federal-jurisdiction strike petitions and legally recognized strikes during the 1989–2010 period only partly conformed to these longer-term historical patterns. The number of strike petitions did not vary consistently with changing economic conditions. Despite the depth of the 1994–5 economic crisis and a strong upturn in inflation, the volume of petitions remained quite constant between 1993 and 1996 (see Table 3). The number of strike petitions did rise substantially in 2008 and 2009 as an international financial crisis pushed Mexico's economy into recession and inflation rose in 2008, but this upturn in the volume of strike petitions actually began in 2004 and thus cannot be attributed solely to more adverse economic conditions. At the same time, the number of legally recognized strikes remained very low from the mid-1990s onward, and it actually declined in 1995 and 2008–09 despite sharply deteriorating economic circumstances.

The data in Table 3 are noteworthy for two additional reasons. First, the overall total of federal-jurisdiction strikes from 1996 onward was lower than it had been since the early 1970s.[33] Second, the strike recognition rate in federal-jurisdiction industries also reached historic lows during the period after 1995. The average recognition rate for the 1963–93 period was 2.2 per cent, with a low of 1.0 per cent in 1973 and a high of 4.2 per cent in 1982. Yet the ratio of strikes to strike petitions was consistently 0.7 per cent or lower between 1996 and 2010, reaching a remarkable 0.1 per cent in 2009 and 2010. The downward shift began during the Zedillo administration (1994–2000), indicating that it was not a consequence of partisan political change at the federal level.

Labour Movement Fragmentation

As the size and political leverage of the 'official' labour movement declined, its organizational fragmentation increased. The Mexican labour movement had long suffered from divisions between larger, more powerful national-industrial unions (such as those industry-wide unions representing petroleum, railroad, mining-metalworking and telephone workers) and the several thousand smaller company- and plant-specific unions grouped in state-level federations. These tensions were often aggravated by rivalries among national confederations such as the CTM, the Revolutionary Confederation of Workers and Peasants (Confederación Revolucionaria de Obreros y Campesinos, CROC), the

---

32 Middlebrook, 1995, pp. 163–9. The correlation between annual variations in strike petitions and the rate of inflation was especially strong in the 1980s.

33 Compare the data in Table 2 with those presented in Middlebrook, 1995, table 5.1.

Mexican Regional Labour Confederation (CROM) and so forth. Such divisions were, however, moderated over time by the formation of umbrella organizations, the Worker Unity Bloc (Bloque de Unidad Obrera) in 1955 and especially the Labour Congress (CT) in 1966. The formation of the CT culminated efforts by Fidel Velázquez Sánchez (who, except for the 1947–50 period, served as the CTM's secretary-general from 1941 until his death in 1997) to unite the labour movement in a single body.[34]

Yet the double pressures of economic restructuring and unions' declining influence within the PRI coalition began, especially after Velázquez's death, to pull the CT apart. 'Official' organizations like the CTM, the CROC, the CROM and major national-industrial unions had long depended on institutional (legal and political) sources of power rather than mobilization, solidarity and coordination among trade unions, or a strong identification between union leaders and rank-and-file members. To the contrary, they were typically characterized by a lack of internal democracy and leaders' top-down control over members. When government policies changed radically, the basic fact that government-allied union leaders were no longer able to deliver customary benefits to their members — combined with their failure to challenge more frontally harsh economic policies and industrial restructuring in the workplace — hurt their credibility and intensified challenges to the CT, whose affiliates' dependence on government subsidies reduced their capacity to respond effectively to dramatically altered economic conditions (Bensusán, 2004, pp. 242–3). One telling indicator of 'official' unions' declining prestige — and their leaders' growing fear that they might no longer be able to control the actions of rank-and-file members — was their decision on three consecutive occasions (1995–7) to cancel the traditional May Day parade in downtown Mexico City (Bizberg, 2003, p. 231).

In the 1990s, two distinct tendencies emerged within the labour movement to rival government-allied unions grouped in the Labour Congress.[35] The first could be characterized as 'social trade unionism', a tendency that combined characteristics of traditional 'business' unionism and 'movement' unionism. Its members were distinguished by their relative autonomy from the state, their effectiveness in negotiating with employers to secure favourable contract terms, and their comparatively strong commitment to internal democracy and meaningful ties between union leaders and their members. The most

---

34 Velázquez was succeeded in the post by Leonardo Rodríguez Alcaine, one of the substitute secretary-generals appointed in the last years of Velázquez's reign and the long-time leader of the General Union of Mexican Electrical Workers (Sindicato Único de Trabajadores Electricistas de la República Mexicana). He served as CTM secretary-general until his death in 2005. Joaquín Gamboa Pascoe, veteran leader of the Federal District Workers' Federation (Federación de Trabajadores del Distrito Federal), succeeded him in 2006.

35 This discussion draws on Bensusán, 2004, pp. 243–5.

prominent exemplars were the Mexican Telephone Workers' Union (Sindicato de Telefonistas de la República Mexicana, STRM), the Mexican Electricians' Union (Sindicato Mexicano de Electricistas, SME) and, more generally, the members of the Federation of Unions of Goods and Services Unions (Federación de Sindicatos de Empresas de Bienes y Servicios, FESEBS) and the National Union of Workers (Unión Nacional de Trabajadores, UNT).[36] The leading force in both the FESEBS (created in 1990) and the UNT (whose organizers purposefully delayed acting until shortly after Velázquez's death in 1997) was STRM secretary-general Francisco Hernández Juárez.[37]

The second rival tendency consisted of 'movement' trade unionism. Its affiliates rejected market-centred economic reforms more overtly than did their 'social trade unionism' counterparts, and they maintained much closer ties with urban popular movements, the women's movement and other social movements. Their organizational structures gave a substantial weight to membership meetings and methods of direct democracy in internal decision making. They also systematically employed mobilizations, strikes or work stoppages in their confrontations with employers and the government. Prominent examples of this tendency included the May 1 Inter-Union Coordinating Network (Coordinadora Inter-sindical Primero de Mayo, CIPM, created in 1995), the Authentic Labour Front (Frente Auténtico del Trabajo, FAT), unions of university employees, and dissident elements within national-industrial unions representing education, electrical power generation and petroleum workers.[38]

Of these new groups, the UNT proved the most consequential rival to the Labour Congress; indeed, it overtly aspired to displace the CT as Mexico's leading labour confederation. The UNT's membership grew in the first years after its formation, but its expansion eventually stalled. As a consequence, in

36 The UNT was founded in November 1997 by 23 unions representing some 325,000 workers (Gatica Lara, 2007, pp. 77–8). Its collective leadership comprised leaders of its three largest affiliates: the STRM, the National Union of Social Security Workers (Sindicato Nacional de Trabajadores del Seguro Social, SNTSS) and the Autonomous National University of Mexico Workers' Union (Sindicato de Trabajadores de la Universidad Nacional Autónoma de México). Neither the SME nor the powerful National Education Workers' Union (SNTE) joined the UNT. On the UNT's origins and goals, see Samstad, 2002, pp. 13–4; Bizberg, 2003, pp. 231–3.

37 Hernández Juárez created the FESEBS in April 1990, but because of CTM opposition it did not receive its official STPS registry until September 1992. In the early 1990s this organization grouped approximately 100,000 workers in the telecommunications, airline, electrical power generation, film and television, tramway and automobile industries (Middlebrook, 1995, p. 296).

38 By 2000 the CIPM had largely disbanded (Sánchez Díaz, 2002, p. 91; Quiroz Trejo, 2004, p. 11). The FAT was formed in 1960 as a Christian Democratic labour organization (Middlebrook, 1995, p. 224; Hathaway, 2000). Despite its small membership, it gained national prominence in the mid-1990s on the basis of its opposition to the North American Free Trade Agreement. It was among the most active Mexican unions engaged in forging collaborative ties with like-minded Canadian and US labour organizations. See Chapter Five.

2008 the Confederation of Mexican Workers remained the country's largest labour confederation. The CTM counted some 608,000 members in federal-jurisdiction industries, as well as a large membership in the heterogeneous state-jurisdiction economic activities organized in the CTM's various federations, for a total membership of approximately one million workers. It held a dominant position in the petroleum, electrical power generation, automobile, steel, sugar and *maquiladora* industries.[39] Nevertheless, the UNT consolidated its position as the principal alternative to the CT in debates over national labour policy (including proposals to reform the Federal Labour Law), thus introducing a degree of political pluralism in the labour movement that had been absent since the late 1940s. By the same token, however, organizational fragmentation and rivalries among groups with different political goals and allegiances prevented the labour movement from speaking with a single voice in national policy debates.[40]

Electoral Democratization and Labour Politics

From the early 1990s onward, democratization challenged the political position of 'official' labour organizations and gradually opened up new opportunities for worker participation and representation, although these changes did not bring about a significant increase in labour's overall policy influence. The CTM, which since 1938 had held a privileged political position as the PRI's official labour sector organization, resisted regime liberalization in the mid-1970s because its leaders feared that legalizing leftist opposition parties and permitting them an expanded presence in the federal Congress (via access to proportional-representation seats in the Chamber of Deputies) might embolden opposition forces to challenge its control over rank-and-file members.[41] In the early 1990s, the CTM successfully blocked internal PRI reforms that threatened to diminish the influence of sectoral organizations in party decision making and reduce their share of elective positions (Middlebrook,

39   García, 2008; Muñoz Rios, 2007; Zapata, 2006, p. 20; Gómez 2010a. In contrast, in 1997 the CTM had 581 affiliated organizations and 926,455 individual members in federal-jurisdiction economic activities alone (Aguilar García, 2001, table V.7; García, 2008).

40   In 1999 the Supreme Court declared unconstitutional those provisions in the Federal Law for Public Service Workers (LFSTE) that barred more than one union in a federal government workplace and required that federal government employees affiliate with the Federation of Public Service Workers' Unions (Federación de Sindicatos de Trabajadores al Servicio del Estado, FSTSE) (Pérez Arce Ibarra, 1999). This decision established the legal basis for a major secession from the FSTSE in 2003, when the National Education Workers' Union (SNTE) led 13 unions and parts of six others out of the FSTSE to found the Democratic Federation of Public Service Workers' Unions (Federación Democrática de Sindicatos de Servidores Públicos, FDSSP) in February 2004, with a membership representing as much as 80 per cent of unionized federal government employees (Sánchez, 2003; Gatica Lara, 2007, p. 74).

41   Middlebrook, 1986, pp. 132–3. For an example of vehement CTM opposition to leftist party involvement in labour conflicts, see La Botz, 1992, pp. 135–40.

1995, pp. 297–8; Samstad, 2002, p. 16). Nevertheless, increasingly intense multiparty electoral competition at both the federal and state levels eventually compelled PRI leaders to reconsider the party's candidate selection procedures in order to field the most viable candidates possible.[42] Except in areas in which a particular union enjoyed special strengths (in some mining districts and in petroleum zones, for example), these developments eroded unions' claims on PRI candidacies.

Throughout the decades in which Mexico's 'party of the Revolution' exercised electoral hegemony, preferential access to elective office represented an important political subsidy and power resource for the leaders of major government-allied unions. During this period, nomination by the party as a candidate for public office essentially guaranteed election to that position, and elective positions at the federal, state and municipal levels were distributed as incentives and rewards to regime supporters.[43] The election of union leaders to public office provided a formal channel for the articulation of labour demands, potentially increased labour organizations' bargaining leverage with government officials and private employers, conferred political and social prestige on the individuals involved (as well as access to considerable patronage resources and opportunities for unlawful enrichment through commissions on government contracts) and symbolically reaffirmed labour's inclusion in Mexico's post-revolutionary governing coalition. The value that labour leaders themselves attached to such positions in large part derived from the fact that relatively few individuals of working-class origin held them. Most of the labour leaders rising to high elective office from the 1930s through the 1970s held

42 Langston, 2010, pp. 309, 327; Samstad, 2002, pp. 16–7. Langston and Morgenstern (2009, pp. 175–6) show that as late as the 1980s, of the PRI's three traditional sectors, the labour sector accounted for the largest average share of PRI federal deputies (22.6 per cent, compared to 12.9 per cent for the peasant sector and 9.8 per cent for the 'popular' sector) elected in the 1982, 1985 and 1988 congressional elections. It also reliably controlled a higher share (19 per cent) of federal legislative districts than the other two PRI sectors combined.

The highly contested 1988 presidential election was a turning point in this regard. It is an open question whether labour leaders in any country could have convinced their members to support a party responsible for years of declining real wages and significant job losses in key industries. The task was no doubt especially difficult in July 1988 because the principal opposition candidate was Cuauhtémoc Cárdenas, heir to his father's (President Lázaro Cárdenas, 1934–40) political legacy of nationalist/statist policies and support for labour rights. Nevertheless, government-allied labour leaders were apparently rather ineffective in mobilizing the sectoral vote in support of the PRI's presidential candidate (Carlos Salinas de Gortari) in the election, and, in an unprecedented reversal of electoral fortunes, 30 out of 101 Labour Congress candidates failed to win election (Middlebrook, 1995, pp. 293–4; Reyes del Campillo, 1990, p. 158).

43 Constitutional reforms in 1932 that prohibited the re-election of governors and the immediate re-election of federal and state legislators and municipal officials were especially important in this regard because they created additional mobility opportunities for worker and peasant leaders during a crucial phase of regime consolidation (Middlebrook, 1995, p. 101).

Table 4. Labour Representation in Mexico's Federal Chamber of Deputies, 1979–2009

	1979	1982	1985	1988	1991	1994	1997	2000	2003	2006	2009
Confederation of Mexican Workers (CTM)	45	50	51	34	36	39	28	12	8	4	8
Revolutionary Confederation of Workers and Peasants (CROC)	11	12	11	11	5	5	3	1	2	2	1
National Union of Workers (UNT)	—	—	—	—	—	—	—	3	1	3	2
Other confederations	4	5	3	5	2	2	3	1	1	1	0
Federation of Public Service Workers' Unions (FSTSE)	9	6	7	4	9	6	6	1	1	1	3
National Education Workers' Union (SNTE)	12	15	14	13	12	12	7	10	12	17	18
Other national industrial unions	9	8	10	6	5	1	1	2	4	2	1
Others	1	0	0	1	0	0	0	1	2	5	3
Total labour representatives	91	96	96	74	69	65	48	31	31	35	36
Labour representatives as a percentage of all federal deputies	22.8	24.0	24.0	14.8	13.8	13.0	9.6	6.2	6.2	7.0	7.2

Sources: Bensusán and Middlebrook, 2012, table 15.4. Authors' calculations are based on data presented in, for 1979–88, Pacheco Méndez and Reyes del Campillo, 1989, Reyes del Campillo, 1990 and Vargas Guzmán, 2001; for 1991–2003, Vargas Guzmán, 2001, database compiled by Rosario Ortiz and Cámara de Diputados official website (http://sitl.diputados.gob.mx); for 2000–09, Dirección General de Apoyo Parlamentario (Cámara de Diputados), database compiled by Rosario Ortiz and Cámara de Diputados official website (http://sitl.diputados.gob.mx); and, for 2009–12, Cámara de Diputados official website (http://sitl.diputados.gob.mx), communication from SNTE national executive committee to the Cámara de Diputados on 12 Nov. 2010 (http://snte.org.mx/?P=editomultim ediafile&Multimedia=1824&Type=1) and authors' database.

Notes: The available data indicate that there was no Chamber of Deputies union representation via political parties other than the Institutional Revolutionary Party (Partido Revolucionario Institucional, PRI) prior to 2000, although some deputies for other parties (especially the Party of the Democratic Revolution [Partido de la Revolución Democrática], PRD) had worked as labour activists at some point during their political careers. The full names of the organizations identified by an acronym in the table are: CROC (Confederación Revolucionaria de Obreros y Campesinos); CTM (Confederación de Trabajadores de México); FSTSE (Federación de Sindicatos de Trabajadores al Servicio del Estado); SNTE (Sindicato Nacional de Trabajadores de la Educación); UNT (Unión Nacional de Trabajadores). An electoral reform in 1987 increased the size of the Chamber of Deputies from 400 to 500 seats.

The CTM total includes: labour representatives from 27 state-level, women's and youth federations; the General Union of Mexican Electrical Workers (Sindicato Único de Trabajadores Electricistas de la República Mexicana); the Mexican Petroleum Workers' Union (Sindicato de Trabajadores Petroleros de la República Mexicana); the Mexican Union of Chemical, Petrochemical and Carbochemical Industry Workers (Sindicato de Trabajadores de la Industria Química y Petroquímica, Carboquímica, Similares y Conexos de la República Mexicana); the Mexican Union of Sugar Industry Workers (Sindicato de Trabajadores de la Industria Azucarera y Similares de la República Mexicana); and the Mexican Union of Television and Radio Workers and Artists (Sindicato Industrial de Trabajadores y Artistas de Televisión y Radio, Similares y Conexos de la República Mexicana).

The UNT total includes: the Autonomous National University of Mexico Workers' Union (Sindicato de Trabajadores de la Universidad Nacional Autónoma de México); the Mexican Telephone Workers' Union (Sindicato de Telefonistas de la República Mexicana) after 1997; and, between 1997 and 2009, the National Union of Social Security Workers (Sindicato Nacional de Trabajadores del Seguro Social).

'Other confederations' includes: the Confederation of Workers and Peasants (Confederación de Trabajadores y Campesinos); General Confederation of Workers (Confederación General de Trabajadores); the Mexican Regional Labour Confederation (Confederación Regional Obrera Mexicana); and the Revolutionary Labour Confederation (Confederación Obrera Revolucionaria).

'Other national industrial unions' includes: the Mexican Electricians' Union (Sindicato Mexicano de Electricistas); the Mexican Mining and Metalworkers' Union (Sindicato Nacional de Trabajadores Mineros, Metalúrgicos y Similares de la República Mexicana); the Mexican Railroad Workers' Union (Sindicato de Trabajadores Ferrocarrileros de la República Mexicana); the National Federation of Bank Unions (Federación Nacional de Sindicatos Bancarios); and, before 1997, the National Union of Social Security Workers (Sindicato Nacional de Trabajadores del Seguro Social).

'Others' includes: the Autonomous University of Guerrero Faculty Union (Unión Sindical de Catedráticos de la Universidad Autónoma de Guerrero); the Autonomous University of Zacatecas Academic Personnel Union (Sindicato del Personal Académico de la Universidad Autónoma de Zacatecas); the Colegio de Bachilleres Faculty Union (Sindicato de Profesores del Colegio de Bachilleres); the Federation of Aviation Sector Unions (Federación de Sindicatos del Sector Aéreo); the General Union of the Autonomous University of Sinaloa (Sindicato Único de la Universidad Autónoma de Sinaloa); the General Union of Hidalgo State Government Workers (Sindicato Único de Trabajadores al Servicio de los Poderes del Estado de Hidalgo); the Harper Whitman de México Workers' Union (Sindicato de Harper Whitman de México); the National Association of Associations and Unions of University Academic Personnel (Asociación Nacional de Asociaciones y Sindicatos de Personal Académico Universitario); the National Union of Airline and Affiliated Workers (Sindicato Nacional de Trabajadores al Servicio de las Líneas Aéreas, Similares y Conexos); National Union of Collective Transport System Workers (Sindicato Nacional de Trabajadores del Sistema de Transporte Colectivo); the Union of Academic Personal of the Autonomous University of the State of Mexico (Sindicato de Personal Académico de la Universidad Autónoma del Estado de México); the University of Guadalajara Academic Workers' Union (Sindicato de Trabajadores Académicos de la Universidad de Guadalajara); and those not identified by name in the available sources.

positions in the federal Chamber of Deputies or in state-level legislatures; only a small number ever held positions in the federal Senate or as state governor.[44]

The Political Representation of Organized Labour

Electoral democratization produced heavy political losses for the CTM, as well as for other Labour Congress-affiliated confederations and even for major national-industrial unions.[45] Table 4 reports the number of union representatives who held seats in the federal Chamber of Deputies between 1979 and 2009.[46] Over this period, the CTM's total number of labour deputies fell dramatically, from a high of 51 in the 1985–8 legislature to a low of just four in 2006–09. Its relative position actually strengthened during the 1990s as other labour organizations initially bore the brunt of declining numbers of PRI-affiliated labour deputies; indeed, the CTM's share of all PRI-affiliated union representatives in the Chamber reached 60 per cent in 1994–7. After 2000, however, even the CTM's relative position declined to a historic low; it controlled only 11.4 per cent of labour deputies in the 2006–09 legislature.[47]

Other CT-affiliated confederations fared even worse than the CTM. The CROC, which had been formed in 1952 with government support as a means of grouping anti-CTM union forces in an organization loyal to the government and which for many years was Mexico's second most important labour confederation, saw its labour delegation in the Chamber shrink from 11 or 12 federal deputies between 1979 and 1988 to one in the 2009–12 legislature (Table 4). The CROM and the General Confederation of Workers (Confederación General de Trabajadores) — an anarcho-syndicalist-inspired confederation originally formed in 1921 which, along with the CROM, had long constituted part of Mexico's 'living museum' of politically marginal labour organizations — had by 2006 disappeared completely from the Chamber of Deputies' labour delegation.[48] Perhaps even more remarkable, the heretofore-powerful federation of federal government employees, the Federation of Public Service Workers' Unions (Federación de Sindicatos de Trabajadores al Servicio del Estado, FSTSE), lost all but one of its representatives in the Chamber

---

44 Middlebrook, 1995, pp. 101–5. Between 1955 and 2010, at least 11 CTM leaders served as governor in the states of Campeche (twice), Durango, Nayarit (twice), Querétaro (twice), Sinaloa (three times) and Zacatecas (Pastrana, 2004).

45 The discussion here and in the following subsection follows Bensusán and Middlebrook, 2012, pp. 346–51.

46 The data in Table 4 for the 1979–97 period refer only to PRI union representatives.

47 Authors' calculations based on data presented in Table 4. Over the period from 1937 to 1973, the CTM's share of all labour representatives in the federal Chamber of Deputies never fell below 50 per cent (in 1970–3) and ranged as high as 95.2 per cent (in 1958–61) (Middlebrook, 1995, table 3.1).

48 These more detailed comments concerning labour representation in the Chamber of Deputies are based on the same sources listed in Table 4.

after 2000 and only recovered a modest presence in 2009. National-industrial unions representing electrical power generation, mining and metalworking, petroleum, railroad and Mexican Social Security Institute (IMSS) workers together held between six and ten seats in the Chamber between 1979 and 1988, but by 2009 this total had fallen to one — fewer seats than the Mexican Mining and Metalworkers' Union (Sindicato Nacional de Trabajadores Mineros, Metalúrgicos y Similares de la República Mexicana, SNTMMSRM) alone had controlled during most of the 1979–91 period.

There were two noteworthy exceptions to this general decline in the representation of labour organizations in the federal Chamber of Deputies. The first was the National Education Workers' Union (SNTE), which consistently maintained a significant presence in the Chamber throughout the 1979–2009 period.[49] Over these three decades it held an average of 13 seats in each three-year legislative period, and between 2003 and 2009 it eclipsed even the CTM as the most prominent labour presence in the Chamber. Its comparative success reflected both the union's continuing appeal as an electoral ally — it was the largest single trade union in Mexico (and, indeed, in all of Latin America) — and its leaders' remarkable success in forging alliances with a broader range of parties than any other labour organization. In fact, in the 2009–12 legislature there were SNTE deputies — albeit from rival union factions — affiliated with the PRI (six); the centre-left Party of the Democratic Revolution (Partido de la Revolución Democrática, PRD; two); the centre-right National Action Party (PAN; two); the Labour Party (Partido del Trabajo, PT; one); and the SNTE's own New Alliance Party (Partido Nueva Alianza, PANAL; seven).

Second, beginning in 2003, a new set of labour actors gained representation in the Chamber of Deputies. Foremost among them were unions representing academic personnel and blue-collar workers at the National Autonomous University of Mexico (Universidad Nacional Autónoma de México) and state-level universities, including universities in Guerrero, Jalisco, the state of México, Sinaloa and Zacatecas.[50] These unions were generally linked to the PRD.

The principal cause of the long-term decline in labour representation in the Chamber of Deputies (over the 1979–2009 period, labour representatives as a proportion of all deputies fell from a high of 24 per cent in 1982 and 1985 to a low of 6.2 per cent in 2000 and 2003, before rising slightly to 7.2 per cent 2009–12; Table 4) lay in the PRI's reduced electoral weight and shifts in its own candidate-selection strategy.[51] Labour as a social force had long

49 We analyse the SNTE case in more detail at the end of this chapter.

50 These unions are grouped under 'Others' in Table 4. The individual names of these unions appear in the accompanying notes.

51 The PRI's share of the valid vote in presidential elections fell from 87.8 per cent in 1964 to 22.7 per cent in 2006. Its share of the valid vote in federal Chamber of Deputies elections fell

been identified with the 'party of the Revolution', and all of the major labour organizations whose presence in the federal Chamber of Deputies declined significantly between 1979 and 2009 had well-established ties to the PRI.[52] Although the National Action Party's victorious candidates won considerable support from union households in the 2000 and 2006 presidential elections (see below), the party had historically been identified more closely with business interests. The PAN did sometimes sponsor labour leaders as congressional candidates (including affiliates of the CTM and the UNT in 2000), and in 2009 it reserved a proportional-representation seat in the Chamber for the leader of the National Union of Social Security Workers (Sindicato Nacional de Trabajadores del Seguro Social, SNTSS) to reward him for his support in the PAN-controlled federal government's successful effort to win major contract concessions regarding pension benefits for Mexican Social Security Institute employees.[53] However, the PAN did not show much sustained interest in building ties to unions.[54] This stance reflected both the resilience of major unions' allegiance to the PRI and, more generally, the limited electoral attractiveness of a shrinking unionized population.

Thus, even after the long decline portrayed in Table 4, the PRI's Chamber delegation in 2009 included more labour representatives (20 deputies, who constituted 55.6 per cent of all labour representatives in the Chamber) than all

from 90.2 per cent in 1961, to 74 per cent in 1979 and to just 28.2 per cent in 2006. Authors' calculations based on data in Gómez Tagle, 1997, tables 2a, 2b, 4, and Instituto Federal Electoral, 2006.

Union representatives held 11.7 per cent of all Senate seats in 1970–6 and 6.3 per cent in 2006–12 (Middlebrook, 1995, table 3.2; www.senado.gob.mx). In this latter period, the SNTE (three senators) and the CTM (two senators) constituted the largest labour presence. Six of the eight labour representatives were distributed among the PRI (three), PAN (one), PRD (one) and the Convergence (Convergencia) party (one); two of the three SNTE members holding Senate seats had no specific party affiliation.

52   The available data indicate that there was no Chamber of Deputies union representation via political parties other than the PRI prior to 2000, although some deputies for other parties (especially the PRD) had worked as labour activists at some point during their political careers.

53   This development produced tensions between other UNT affiliates (who were generally aligned politically with the PRD) and the SNTSS, whose approximately 300,000 members were by far the largest force in the UNT. In 2010 the SNTSS finally withdrew from the UNT, dealing an exceptionally serious blow to the largest grouping of politically independent trade unions.

54   The exceptional case of the SNTE and the New Alliance Party is discussed later in this chapter.
One of the few known efforts to foment an alliance between labour groups and the PAN occurred in May 1999 at the First National Encounter of PAN Worker Unionists in Juriquilla, Querétaro. The meeting brought together some 200 unionists (mainly public-sector employees) from 27 states. The Sinaloa and Tlaxcala delegations called for the creation of a PAN-allied labour federation. However, this initiative was opposed by PAN senator Francisco Javier Salazar Sáenz (one of the meeting's principal organizers and minister of labour and social welfare in 2005–06), who argued that official links to political parties were 'a very evil threat' to unionism. *Mexican Labor News and Analysis*, vol. 4, no. 10 (June 1999).

other parties combined. Union representatives constituted a larger proportion of the PRI's Chamber of Deputies delegation (8.4 per cent) than any other major party's (PT, 7.7 per cent; PRD, 4.3 per cent; PAN, 3.5 per cent).[55]

Union Members at the Polls

As a consequence of electoral democratization, rank-and-file union members gained expanded scope for individual political choice. Strong multiparty competition may have at times enhanced the CTM's lobbying leverage within the PRI, for which workers' votes became relatively more important in close electoral contests. Moreover, some major unions (including those representing education, mining-metalworking and petroleum workers) retained considerable capacity to mobilize their members behind particular parties and candidates. In general, however, the gradual consolidation by the mid-1990s of institutional reforms ensuring free and fair electoral processes (especially in federal elections) made it more difficult for union bosses to control their members' behaviour in the voting booth, especially in large cities where union members were widely dispersed among a heterogeneous urban population.[56]

Unionized workers' partisan identifications reflected shifts in the sociological composition of the labour movement and growing political pluralism in Mexico as the PRI's hegemony weakened after the mid-1990s.[57] National

55 Authors' calculations based on data from the sources listed in Table 4. The New Alliance Party was again the exception; 70 per cent of its federal deputies were affiliated with the SNTE.

The differences in this regard among Mexico's three major parties were not proportional to their share of all Chamber of Deputies seats. In 2009 the PRI controlled 47.4 per cent of all Chamber seats, while the PAN and the PRD held 28.6 per cent and 13.8 per cent, respectively.

56 The landmark 1996 Federal Code of Electoral Institutions and Procedures (Código Federal de Instituciones y Procedimientos Electorales) prohibited collective affiliation to political parties, which had long been stipulated in the statutes of many PRI-linked unions (Ramírez Sáiz, 2003, p. 140).

For a dissent from the conventional view that PRI-affiliated unions were effective at mobilizing workers' electoral support, see Davis, 1989, pp. 109, 124–5, 128, 143, 147–8, 153.

57 Similar changes were evident in unionized workers' policy views and ideological self-placement. Union membership still correlated strongly with the positions that workers held on some major public policy issues. However, although a strong majority of union households surveyed in 2000 were opposed to privatizing state-owned enterprises (61 per cent, compared to 54.3 per cent of blue-collar workers and 52 per cent of survey respondents in general), a substantial proportion of union households (29.6 per cent) expressed support for this policy (Lawson et al., 2000, Wave 1, question 29, N = 2,263). Similarly, although 54.8 per cent of union households participating in a 2006 electoral survey advocated continued government ownership of the electrical power industry (compared to 54.3 per cent of survey respondents in general), fully 31 per cent supported more private investment in the sector (Lawson et al., 2006, Wave 1, question 43, N = 1,566). A majority of union households participating in the 2006 survey also supported expanded trade with the United States (56.6 per cent) and advocated that individuals, rather than the government, take responsibility for their own economic well-being (54.2 per cent), proportions similar to — or even greater than — survey

election surveys conducted in 2000 and 2006 found that members of union households were still more likely to identify with the PRI (40.8 per cent in 2000 and 29.2 per cent in 2006) than non-union survey respondents (35.8 per cent in 2000; 26.4 per cent in 2006). They were also less inclined to identify with the centre-right PAN (17.3 per cent in 2000 and 22.6 per cent in 2006) than non-union respondents (22.7 per cent in 2000; 23.2 per cent in 2006).[58]

Nevertheless, the PRI's advantage in expressed partisan preferences was remarkably small, and the share of PRI identifiers among union households fell significantly over the 2000–06 period at the same time that the proportion of PAN identifiers increased. Nor did survey data suggest that union households had transferred their partisan support from the PRI to the centre-left PRD (the product of a major split within the PRI in 1987–9). In 2000, at a time when the party's presidential candidate was the PRD founder Cuauhtémoc Cárdenas Solórzano, only 7.2 per cent of union households identified with the PRD (compared to 8.6 per cent of non-union survey respondents), a share that rose modestly to 13.7 per cent in 2006 (compared to 16.9 per cent of the non-union sample). In fact, a very substantial proportion of union households (29.6 per cent in 2000 and 30.4 per cent in 2006, compared to 28.5 and 30.3 per cent, respectively, of non-union respondents) declined to indicate any particular partisan affiliation.[59]

These changes were evident in union members' reported voting behaviour in the highly competitive 2000 and 2006 presidential elections.[60] Bivariate

respondents in general (Lawson et al., 2006, Wave 1, questions 46 [N = 1,566] and 51 [N = 1,566]).

Indeed, national surveys conducted in 2000 and 2006 found that, when members of union households were asked to place themselves on a left-right scale, their views stretched across the entire ideological spectrum. In 2000, 16 per cent of union household members placed themselves on the left (points 0–4), 26.8 per cent at the centre (point 5) and 57.3 per cent on the right (points 6–10) of a ten-point ideological scale, compared to, respectively, 20 per cent, 22.7 per cent and 57.3 per cent of non-union household members (Lawson et al., 2000, Wave 1, question 42, N = 1,622). The 2006 survey, employing a seven-point scale, found that 22 per cent of union-household respondents placed themselves on the left, 27.4 per cent in the centre (combining the positions defined as centre-left, centre-centre and centre-right) and 17.9 per cent on the right, compared to, respectively, 18.4 per cent, 28.5 per cent and 16.3 per cent of the sample as a whole (Lawson et al., 2006, Wave 1, question 73, N = 1,566; fully 14.9 per cent of union-household respondents reported no ideological preference and 17.9 per cent refused to answer the question).

58 Lawson et al., 2000, Wave 1, question 52, N = 2,263; Lawson et al., 2006, Wave 1, question 22, N = 1,566. Lawson et al., 2006 include responses from both individual union members and survey participants from union households (that is, cases in which the respondent or her or his spouse or partner reported being a union member). In order to enhance comparability over the 2000–06 period, this discussion reports only results for union households unless there were notable differences in the responses of the two groups.

59 Lawson et al., 2000, Wave 1, question 52; Lawson et al., 2006, Wave 1, question 22.

60 The text presents results from bivariate analysis. Multinomial logit and multinomial probit estimation was employed to verify the significance of these findings. The regression models for

analysis shows that in the historic July 2000 presidential election that ended the PRI's 71-year control over the federal executive, members of union households did vote for the PRI's Francisco Labastida Ochoa in a higher proportion (39.7 per cent) than the non-union survey sample (29.7 per cent).[61] In contrast, the PAN's charismatic candidate, Vicente Fox Quesada, received more support from non-union households (38.9 per cent) than from union households (32.4 per cent).[62]

However, in the bitterly fought 2006 presidential contest, in which the incumbent PAN retained control over the federal executive by defeating the PRD's Andrés Manuel López Obrador by the slimmest of margins, a higher percentage of union household members reported supporting the PAN's Felipe Calderón Hinojosa (34.4 per cent) than either López Obrador (33.3 per cent) or the PRI's Roberto Madrazo Pintado (23.7 per cent). The proportion of union households that reported backing Madrazo did exceed the support he received from non-union survey respondents (17.8 per cent), and Calderón's reported support among union households was considerably weaker than among non-union respondents (41.5 per cent).[63] Nevertheless, in contrast to the 2000

both the 2000 and 2006 presidential elections employed the winner (Vicente Fox Quesada in 2000, Felipe Calderón Hinojosa in 2006) as the reference candidate. The independent variables included respondents' gender, age, urban/rural residence, strength of religious sentiment, party identification, approval of the incumbent president, income level, left-right ideological alignment, educational attainment and union status (whether or not the respondent was a member of a union household). Cluster-robust standard errors were estimated in all instances.

61 Multivariate analysis confirmed this finding. In the multinomial probit regression, the coefficient of the variable indicating union household support for the PRI candidate, Francisco Labastida Ochoa, was positive (0.399), with a one-tailed P value (a measure of statistical significance) of 0.047 (below the 0.05 threshold customarily employed to establish statistical significance in regression analyses). For a 'typical' respondent (holding other variables at their median values), union households were approximately nine per cent more likely to support Labastida than Fox. A one-tailed test is deemed appropriate in this instance because there is a strong a priori expectation that union households would support the PRI candidate. Older voters, residents of rural areas, respondents indicating partisan identification with the PRI (and rejection of the PAN) and those indicating support for PRI incumbent President Ernesto Zedillo also voted for Labastida in statistically significant higher proportions. Multinomial logistic regression results were very similar.

62 Lawson et al., 2000, Wave 4, question 12, N = 1,216. Members of union households also reported voting somewhat disproportionately for the PRD's Cárdenas (11.3 per cent, compared to 10.9 per cent of the non-union sample) and the Social Democratic Party's (Partido Social Demócrata) Gilberto Rincón Gallardo (2.6 per cent versus 1.4 per cent). Reported abstention rates were also somewhat lower for union households (7.3 per cent) than the non-union sample (12.6 per cent).

63 Lawson et al., 2006, Wave 3, question 6, N = 859. In this instance, the reported behaviour of union members differed somewhat from that of union households. A higher proportion of union members backed López Obrador (37.7 per cent) than Calderón (30.4 per cent), with only 20.3 per cent supporting Madrazo (Lawson et al., 2006, Wave 3, question 6).
    In the 2006 presidential election, a larger percentage of union households (5.4 per cent) supported the Social Democratic and Peasant Alternative Party's (Partido Alternativa Socialdemócrata y Campesina) Patricia Mercado Castro than non-union survey respondents

election, multinomial logistic and probit analyses found that support from union households did not provide Madrazo with any statistically significant advantage over Calderón.[64]

The National Education Workers' Union and the Politics of Leverage

No union adapted more successfully to the challenges posed, and the opportunities offered, by electoral democratization in Mexico than did the National Education Workers' Union. The SNTE, formed in 1943, had for many years been a bulwark of the ruling PRI, its status as Mexico's largest union making it particularly valuable as an electoral ally. In 1989 President Salinas de Gortari responded to the political pressures created by a massive rank-and-file protest movement by forcing the resignation of Carlos Jonguitud Barrios, who had ruled the union since 1974. At least initially, the new union secretary-general, Elba Esther Gordillo Morales, was better positioned than her predecessor to negotiate with the National Coordinating Committee of Education Workers (Coordinadora Nacional de Trabajadores de la Educación, CNTE, formed in 1979), the internal opposition movement that had aggressively promoted union democracy, higher wages and teachers' rights since the late 1970s.[65] Over time, however, Gordillo proved to be just as much of an old-style boss as Jonguitud Barrios; in 2007 la maestra installed herself as the union's 'president for life' (presidenta vitalicia).[66] Her tight control over many important state-level SNTE sections and the union's substantial financial resources, her legendary political pragmatism, and her skill at forging diverse partisan alliances made Gordillo an extremely effective political operator.[67]

(2.1 per cent). However, despite the prominence of teachers among unionized workers, union household support for the PANAL's Roberto Campa Cifrián (1.1 per cent) barely exceeded his support among non-union survey respondents (0.8 per cent).

64   Although the coefficient for the union-household variable was strongly positive in the multinomial probit analysis (.461, with 'education' coded as a series of dummy variables for each educational level attained), its one-tailed P value was 0.081. The only variables giving Madrazo a statistically significant advantage over Calderón were those representing partisan identification with the PRI (and opposition to the PAN) and voters with a negative evaluation of President Vicente Fox. A multinomial logit analysis produced generally comparable results. Statistical analyses of individual union members' support for Madrazo also yielded similar results.

65   On the CNTE, see especially Hernández Navarro, 2011.

66   Delegates to an extraordinary national congress held in March 2004 established the positions of president and secretary-general in the SNTE's national executive committee. Gordillo was elected president in 2004 and re-elected in 2007, with the possibility of indefinite renewals in the post.

67   For details on Gordillo's lengthy political career, see Gatica Lara, 2007, p. 74; see also Cano and Aguirre, 2007; Raphael, 2007; Muñoz Armenta, 2010. Aguayo Quezada and Serdán, 2009 and Raphael, 2007, p. 254 present data on the SNTE's substantial financial resources. The CNTE, which was politically aligned with the PRD, had a strong presence in state-level SNTE sections in Chiapas, the Federal District, Guerrero, Michoacán and Oaxaca (Sánchez, 2010). On the SNTE's broader political role after 2000, see Bensusán and Tapia, 2011.

The splintering of the Labour Congress and the PRI's electoral defeat in 2000 substantially enhanced SNTE autonomy. One measure of the SNTE's growing independence was its decision to secede from the FSTSE in 2004 and form the Democratic Federation of Public Service Workers' Unions (Federación Democrática de Sindicatos de Servidores Públicos, FDSSP). However, it was the union's (and Gordillo's) role in the closely fought 2006 presidential election that demonstrated just how important a place the SNTE held in Mexico's highly competitive electoral democracy (Aguayo Quezada and Serdán, 2009).

In the course of a protracted struggle over position and influence within the PRI in the run-up to the election, Gordillo broke with the party and founded her own political vehicle, the New Alliance Party, in February 2005.[68] The SNTE's educated, well-organized and nationally distributed membership (numbering at least 700,000 in 2010, with as many as 10,000 members dedicated to union-related and political activities) made it a particularly potent electoral force.[69] In an extremely tight contest — the PAN's Calderón (with 36.7 per cent of the valid vote) defeated the PRD's López Obrador (with 36.1 per cent of the valid vote) by just 233,831 of the 41,557,430 ballots cast in the race — the SNTE's support made a significant difference. In fact, Gordillo instructed union members to split their ballots in order to support Calderón's presidential candidacy and still elect PANAL candidates to federal and state legislative seats.[70]

In state and local elections held in July 2010, the SNTE leadership again demonstrated its extreme political pragmatism and the union's electoral effectiveness. In gubernatorial races, the union was aligned with the equally pragmatic Mexican Ecologist Green Party (Partido Verde Ecologista de México, PVEM) and the PRI in eight states, with the PAN in two states, and with both the PAN and the PRD in another state.[71] Only in Oaxaca did the PANAL field its own gubernatorial candidate, who late in the race resigned in favour of the candidate representing what proved to be a victorious anti-PRI coalition — even though the party's national leadership had indicated earlier that it

68 One indicator of the extent of Gordillo's personal influence over the PANAL was the election of her former private secretary and her daughter as, respectively, the party's president and secretary-general in June 2011 (Díaz, 2011).

69 Aguayo Quezada, 2010; Del Valle, 2010a. Vargas Márquez (2006) estimated the SNTE's membership at 1.35 million in 2005. The data gathered by Lawson et al., 2006 (Wave 1, question 62, N = 1,566) suggest that teachers constituted more than one-fifth (22.1 per cent) of all union members in Mexico in 2006.

70 As a consequence, PANAL presidential candidate Roberto Campa received approximately 401,000 votes, while the party's candidates for simple-majority seats in the federal Chamber of Deputies received some 1.27 million votes and its Senate candidates received approximately 1.47 million votes (La Jornada en línea, 13 July 2011, p. 5).

71 Many analysts argue that the PVEM is less a political party than a family enterprise. See, for example, Preciado, 2011.

would support the PRI's candidate.[72] In the view of some analysts, the SNTE's capacity to affect the outcome in tight races such as Oaxaca made Gordillo the principal winner in the 2010 elections (Del Valle, 2010b).

Gordillo and the SNTE reaped substantial benefits from the union's demonstrated electoral leverage. Wages and fringe benefits rose significantly over the 2000–06 period.[73] In 2006 the PANAL won sufficient seats in the Congress (nine seats in the federal Chamber of Deputies) and in state and local government to exercise a significant voice on educational policy issues.[74] Despite the public controversy provoked by the appointment, Gordillo succeeded in having her son-in-law named under-secretary of basic education at the outset of the Calderón administration.[75] Through other favourable personnel appointments, Gordillo and her allies also gained de facto control over the Social Security Institute for State Workers (Instituto de Seguridad y Servicios Sociales de los Trabajadores del Estado, ISSSTE), the cash-rich National Lottery and the Federal District's Federal Administration of Educational Services.[76] In addition, the union's political strength permitted it to resist successfully repeated attempts to reform workplace practices in Mexico's public education system, including regulations that would open teaching appointments to competitive application (thus ending the long-established union practice whereby retiring teachers sell their positions to incoming union members without competitive review).[77] More generally, the administration of President Felipe Calderón

72 Sánchez and Jiménez, 2010. The PANAL itself significantly increased its presence in state legislatures and local municipal councils in 2010; see the data available on the Cámara de Diputados web site (http://sitl.diputados.gob.mx/LXI_leg/info_diputados.php).

73 Bensusán and Tapia (2011, p. 20) calculate that the salary of a first-year primary school teacher rose by 38 per cent in nominal terms between 2000 and 2006.

74 In 2009 a PANAL deputy served as president of the Chamber of Deputies' Commission on Science and Technology. Gordillo and her allies exercised particularly strong influence over educational policy in the states of Campeche, Coahuila, Colima, Nayarit, Quintana Roo and Tabasco (Aguayo Quezada, 2010).

75 In a subsequent defence of her 2006 pact with Calderón and the PAN, Gordillo explained that '... we reached an agreement to back Calderón for the presidency, based on prior arrangements of a political character that should not shame anyone. I am certainly not ashamed of them; I do politics.' Quoted in Avilés, 2011a.

76 Raphael, 2007, pp. 298–9; Aguayo Quezada, 2010. In fact, Gordillo's control over some key federal offices dated from the administration of President Vicente Fox (2000–06), when she first negotiated an electoral alliance with the PAN. Calderón defended the arrangement on the grounds that it was part of a pact with the SNTE to improve the quality of education in Mexico (Cantú, 2011; Loaeza, 2011).

77 Despite her very considerable political clout, Gordillo was unable to block government recognition of a rival teachers' union. In January 2011 the Federal Conciliation and Arbitration Tribunal granted legal recognition to the Independent Union of Mexican Education Workers (Sindicato Independiente de Trabajadores de la Educación de México). Its approximately 7,500 members were located primarily in the states of Guanajuato, Hidalgo, Puebla, Querétaro, Quintana Roo and Veracruz and in the Mexico City area (Avilés, 2011b).

(2006–12) deferred to Gordillo by ignoring a long history of internal SNTE conflicts and denunciations of corruption in the management of union dues and paid leave for union delegates.[78]

The SNTE example underscores, then, the extent to which powerful sectoral interests — the historical product of the concentrated political power that characterized Mexico's post-revolutionary authoritarian regime — continue to influence contemporary affairs. Indeed, one of the most contradictory aspects of democratization in Mexico is precisely that intense multiparty electoral competition has increased the political leverage of some groups closely linked to the *ancien régime*. The SNTE was nonetheless exceptional in its capacity to translate union size and organizational strength into direct influence over public policy during the PAN-led federal administrations that held power after 2000. What was more common was for labour organizations like the Confederation of Mexican Workers to deploy their (much-reduced) political influence to attempt to block policy reforms that threatened their position. However, even when these efforts were successful, they did not reverse the long-term erosion of labour power.[79] It was in fact the fragmentation of the

78 In March 2010, for example, an investigation by the Federal Audit Authority (Auditoría Superior de la Federación) found evidence of corruption in the paid leave the Ministry of Public Education (Secretaría de Educación Pública) provided to 670 workers. On this case and other instances of union corruption, see Martínez, 2008; Cuenca, 2010; Tuckman, 2011.

Nevertheless, Gordillo's relationship with Calderón soured in the political manoeuvring that preceded the 2012 presidential election. In June 2011 Gordillo held a sensational press conference in which she revealed details concerning her 2006 electoral pact with the PAN and accused Miguel Ángel Yunes Linares, previously head of the ISSSTE and formerly her political ally, of extensive corruption in office (Avilés, 2011b, 2011c). These developments did not, however, prevent the PANAL from pragmatically endorsing President Calderón's sister, Luisa María Calderón, as gubernatorial candidate in his home state of Michoacán (Martínez Elorriaga, 2011).

79 The shifting terms of union influence over modifications in social welfare policy further illustrate this point. In the debate preceding the creation of the privately funded Retirement Saving System (SAR) in 1992, the CT (and especially the CTM) vigorously maintained its long-standing support for Mexico's public pension system and offered several alternative proposals for addressing the deepening budgetary problems of the Mexican Social Security Institute (IMSS), including measures to increase administrative efficiency, enhance employers' compliance with their IMSS obligations and increase employers' overall financial contributions to pension programmes. Leaders of the CTM also called on the government to establish national unemployment insurance, and they argued that individual retirement accounts should be managed by the Worker Bank (BO) rather than by commercial banks or other private financial firms. The CTM did not achieve either of these latter goals, but it did succeed temporarily in preserving the integrity of IMSS pension programmes and in influencing the scope of the SAR (Bertranou, 1995, pp. 11–9).

In contrast, the CT played a negligible role in negotiations over the privatization of pensions for Social Security Institute for State Workers (ISSSTE) affiliates in 2007. Instead, the key players were the National Education Workers' Union (SNTE) and the Federation of Public Service Workers' Unions (FSTSE). The largest concession that labour negotiators achieved was to make the requirement of individual retirement accounts mandatory only for those workers who would become ISSSTE affiliates after the revised legislation took effect,

labour movement and the declining influence of the Labour Congress and the CTM that expanded the political opportunities available to the SNTE and other influential sector-specific unions.

thus preserving the right of workers who were employed at the time the measure was adopted to choose between the (arguably more favourable) old or new pension schemes. However, the main beneficiaries were SNTE leader Elba Esther Gordillo and private financial institutions. The SNTE and the newly created Democratic Federation of Public Service Workers' Unions (FDSSP) gained significant representation on the governing board of PENSIONISSSTE, the organization created to manage public-sector workers' pension contributions. Private financial institutions won authorization to manage individual retirement accounts after they have been lodged with PENSIONISSSTE for a three-year period (Aziz, 2007; Centro de Estudios de las Finanzas Públicas, 2007; Leal, 2007).

Chapter Four
The Limits of Democratization: Labour Politics During the Fox and Calderón Administrations

The National Action Party's (PAN) victory in the July 2000 presidential election opened a new political era in Mexico. Almost immediately, however, the incoming administration of President Vicente Fox Quesada (2000–06) recognized that the historic alliance between major labour unions and the former ruling party, the Institutional Revolutionary Party (PRI), posed a potentially severe challenge. Indeed, one of the central questions in the general uncertainty accompanying regime change was whether PRI-allied unions would unleash a wave of strikes in an attempt to destabilize the new government and deal the PAN an early political defeat. Among other negative consequences for the Fox administration, extensive worker unrest could have dissuaded transnational companies from making the investments required to generate economic growth and employment.

Even before he formally assumed office on 1 December 2000, Fox sought to avoid these risks by reaching a modus vivendi with the Confederation of Mexican Workers (CTM) and other unions grouped in the Labour Congress (CT) (Bensusán, 2005a, pp. 117–18; La Botz, 2000; Monroy Aguirre, 2000). Like preceding PRI governments, the Fox administration found itself dependent on old-guard labour leaders' willingness to control rank-and-file demands in exchange for government support. Fox administration labour officials were in fact surprised by how quickly these union leaders adapted to a new political reality — albeit one in which both parties reaffirmed that long-established understandings in state-labour relations would remain in force.[1] The government's strategic decision to ally itself with CT affiliates did,

---

1   Middlebrook interview with a former Fox administration labour official, 10 July 2008, Mexico City.

however, force it to set aside ambitious proposals to recast state-labour relations as part of broad democratic change.[2]

Indeed, far from initiating a democratic transformation of the existing state-labour relations regime, in practice both the Fox government and the succeeding PAN administration led by President Felipe Calderón Hinojosa (2006–12) relied heavily on legal controls over unions to punish labour opponents and implement pro-business policies. High-profile, protracted conflicts with the Mexican Mining and Metalworkers' Union (SNTMMSRM) and the Mexican Electricians' Union (SME) forcefully underscored the ways in which the legacies of Mexico's authoritarian past continued to shape labour politics even after the consolidation of electoral democracy.

Following a detailed examination of these emblematic conflicts, this chapter analyses attempts by the Fox and Calderón administrations between 2001 and 2011 to reform Mexico's Federal Labour Law (LFT). Although the political circumstances surrounding reform episodes in 2001–02 and 2010–11 differed greatly, the alignment of contending political forces remained much the same. In the first instance, the Party of the Democratic Revolution (PRD) and its principal labour ally, the National Union of Workers (UNT), sought to exploit the democratic opening created by Fox's election victory and revise the LFT in ways that would have reduced state intervention in union affairs and strengthened democratic accountability in union governance. In contrast, the Fox administration's business supporters and its new-found allies in the Labour Congress lobbied for a reform proposal that addressed employers' demands for enhanced hiring and contract flexibility and managerial discretion in workplace relations, while simultaneously preserving the collective-rights provisions in the LFT that underpinned the entrenched position of old-guard union leaders.

In the second episode, the policy positions adopted by the PRD, the PAN, and their respective labour allies remained largely unchanged, but the PRI's tactical calculations differed significantly. Rather than being on the political defensive in the immediate aftermath of Fox's historic presidential victory, in 2010–11 the party held the decisive bloc of votes in the federal Chamber of Deputies and was strongly favoured to regain control of the presidency in 2012. PRI legislators initially produced a rather progressive proposal for labour law reform. However, as party leaders manoeuvred to appeal to the business community for its political support while still maintaining the allegiance of Labour Congress affiliates, the PRI soon altered course and backed the more conservative, business-friendly policy initiatives long espoused by the PAN.

---

2   On 7 June 2000 Fox and reform-minded union leaders had signed a document titled 'Twenty Commitments for Union Freedom and Democracy' ('Veinte compromisos para la libertad y la democracia sindical, para el cumplimiento de los derechos individuales y colectivos y para la agenda laboral y el programa de gobierno'). See Alcalde Justiniani et al., 2003, pp. 223–7.

The PAN in Power: The Fox and Calderón Administrations Confront Miners and Electrical Workers

The labour policies adopted by the two PAN governments that held power between 2000 and 2012 changed significantly over time. Under Carlos Abascal Carranza, head of the Ministry of Labour and Social Welfare (STPS) between 2000 and 2005, the Fox administration took a relatively balanced position in worker-employer relations. Abascal was himself a devout, conservative Catholic, and the liberal press excoriated him for undermining Mexico's long-established secular traditions by promoting religious values (and the interests of the Roman Catholic Church) in public life.[3] However, Abascal had also been associated since 1995 with efforts to promote a more consensual 'new labour culture' (*nueva cultura laboral*) that would reduce worker-employer hostility and reward increased labour productivity, and as president of the Mexican Employers' Confederation (Confederación Patronal de la República Mexicana, COPARMEX) he had negotiated extensively with the CTM's Fidel Velázquez in order to advance these goals (Bensusán, 2000, pp. 418–21; Confederación de Trabajadores de México, 1996).

Under Abascal's direction, the STPS actively sought to mediate labour conflicts, but government officials did not automatically back employers or use their legal authority to undercut unions' bargaining positions. At least initially, the STPS recognized the political importance of independent labour groups by formally including the UNT in 2001–02 roundtable negotiations over labour law reform. (UNT representatives accounted for three of the 11 union members on the STPS-coordinated employer-worker commission charged with negotiating a consensus labour law reform proposal.) Government labour officials also sought to protect workers' income by backing minimum-wage increases that were at least marginally above the prevailing rate of inflation.[4]

In June 2005, however, Abascal resigned as minister of labour and took up the more politically influential post of minister of the interior. His replacement at the STPS was Francisco Javier Salazar Sáenz, who had previously served as the leader of a university employees' union in San Luis Potosí, a federal deputy and senator for the PAN, and a senior STPS official under Abascal.[5]

---

3   In 2001, for example, Abascal urged business and union leaders to adopt principles of Christian solidarity in worker-employer relations (De la Garza, 2003, p. 352n8).

4   See Bensusán, 2005a, pp. 111–12; De la Garza, 2003, p. 352; Table 1 (Chapter Three, above). Several leaders of major independent unions recognized the significance of these policies (Mayer, 2006).

5   Salazar was secretary-general of the Union of Academic Personnel Associations of the Autonomous University of San Luis Potosí (Unión de Asociaciones de Personal Académico de la Universidad Autónoma de San Luis Potosí) between 1979 and 1985, and secretary-general of the National Confederation of University Workers (Confederación Nacional de Trabajadores Universitarios) during 1987–90 (Camp, 2011, p. 864).

Both Salazar and Javier Lozano Alarcón, his successor at the STPS from 2006 through 2011, adopted a far more conservative policy stance. Indeed, whereas in opposition the National Action Party had criticized undue state interference in union affairs, in government it now freely made use of the extensive legal controls over unions that it inherited from the authoritarian regime the PAN had opposed since its founding in 1939.[6] At times the STPS's discretionary actions and its efforts to undercut elected union leaders who challenged government policies were counterbalanced by a more independent judiciary. On the whole, though, the government retained broad discretion in the handling of such matters as the certification of union elections.[7] As bitter conflicts involving the SNTMMSRM and the SME amply demonstrated, the key beneficiaries of this policy stance were the PAN's big-business allies.

The Mine Workers' Conflict

Near the end of the Fox administration, two events occurred in the mining industry that would have high social and economic costs for all those involved. Together they underscored the pro-business orientation of the PAN's labour policies, the government's willingness to exploit for its own political ends the internal weaknesses of union opponents (while ignoring similar defects in its union allies) and the serious obstacles that workers faced in securing timely and impartial justice.

First, on 17 February 2006, the STPS arbitrarily displaced the national executive committee of the Mexican Mining and Metalworkers' Union, headed by Napoleón Gómez Urrutia.[8] He had attained his position of union secretary-general by succeeding his father, Napoleón Gómez Sada, who had

6   For example, in June 2000 PAN presidential candidate Vicente Fox had promised 'to eliminate the [union] registration requirement and recognition [of elected union leaders] by labour authorities, and to establish a public registry of unions and collective contracts. The agency responsible for the registration [of unions and contracts] will be public and autonomous of the federal executive.' Quoted in Alcalde Justiniani et al., 2003, p. 17.

7   Government officials can gain political advantage not only by refusing to recognize the election of labour opponents, as the SNTMMSRM and SME cases demonstrated, but also by granting recognition to union allies on arbitrarily favourable terms. For example, in November 2010 the Ministry of Labour and Social Welfare's Associational Registry recognized the re-election of Valdemar Gutiérrez Fragoso, secretary-general of the National Union of Social Security Workers (SNTSS), for the 2012–18 period even before his old term had expired. The STPS's action contravened the union's statutes, which explicitly prohibit the re-election of union officials. Moreover, the STPS authorized Gutiérrez — on an exceptional basis that was supposedly not to set a precedent — to appoint the other members of the new SNTSS national executive committee (Tribunal Internacional de Libertad Sindical, 2011, point X). As noted in Chapter Three, Gutiérrez had won favour with the Calderón administration by agreeing to a controversial modification of the pension plan for Mexican Social Security Institute (IMSS) employees.

8   This discussion draws in part on SNTMMSRM and government documents summarized in International Labour Organization (ILO), 2008b. See also Centro de Acción y Reflexión Laboral, 2007, pp. 36–9.

ruled the miners' union with an iron hand from 1960 until illness forced him to relinquish control in 2000. Gómez Urrutia had received a postgraduate degree in economics from the University of Oxford and subsequently served as director of the Casa de la Moneda (Mexico's national mint). He had not, however, worked as a mine employee or been a union member during the five years prior to his election to the union leadership — a clear violation of the SNTMMSRM's statutes. Nevertheless, even though the PRI-controlled STPS had on this basis rejected Gómez Sada's attempt to install his son as adjunct secretary-general in April–August 2000, in 2001 STPS Secretary Abascal ratified Gómez Urrutia's initial election as secretary-general (Rendón Corona, 2005, pp. 189–91; Sarmiento, 2008).

In contrast, Francisco Javier Salazar, Abascal's successor at the STPS, used the same arbitrary administrative authority to remove Gómez Urrutia from the union leadership, evidently because he had taken a series of positions at odds with the interests of the Fox administration and its political allies. He had, for instance, opposed Abascal's proposal for labour law reform in 2002 and encouraged the PRI's congressional delegation to block discussion of the legislative initiative. Gómez Urrutia had also dissented from the re-election of Víctor Flores Morales, secretary-general of the Mexican Railroad Workers' Union (Sindicato de Trabajadores Ferrocarrileros de la República Mexicana), as head of the Labour Congress in February 2006. His greatest 'sin', though, had been to resist the restrictive wage policies adopted by the federal government and mining companies, organizing numerous strikes and work stoppages to pressure companies into conceding higher salaries at a time when mining firms were earning enormous profits because of rapidly rising international mineral prices. This unprecedented level of mobilization by a union long allied with the PRI (Gómez Urrutia's father had rarely led strikes or work stoppages during his long tenure as union leader) won Gómez Urrutia substantial support from rank-and-file union members. However, it also incurred the wrath of employers like Grupo México, the country's largest mining consortium and a beneficiary of high-level support from President Fox and his wife, Marta.[9]

In its action on 17 February, the STPS's Associational Registry backed a challenge to Gómez Urrutia and the incumbent SNTMMSRM executive committee that had been lodged by two members of the union's General Vigilance and Justice Council. The underlying charge was that Gómez Urrutia and his closest collaborators had embezzled money from a US$55 million union trust fund established to benefit workers following the 1991 privatization of the Cananea mine, Mexico's largest (and the world's third largest) copper mine.[10]

9   Grupo México executives were important contributors to Marta Sahagún de Fox's Fundación Vamos México ('Let's Go, Mexico' Foundation) (Vergara, 2006).

10   ILO, 2008b, point 1292. Ironically, it was Gómez Urrutia who had compelled the company to honour its commitment to establish this trust fund.

Gómez Urrutia protested his innocence, and he demonstrated continued rank-and-file support by winning the endorsement of two separate SNTMMSRM conventions in March and May 2006.[11] The entire process was, moreover, riddled with evidence of political manipulation. (For example, one of the two vigilance council officials named as original complainants later confirmed to legal authorities that his signature on the complaint had been falsified.)[12] Nevertheless, the government froze the union's bank accounts and, despite losing a series of court decisions, federal and state officials repeatedly issued arrest warrants for Gómez Urrutia.[13]

Whatever the merits of the specific legal charges against Gómez Urrutia, the government's clear political goal — doggedly pursued first by the Fox administration and then by the Calderón administration — was to divide and weaken the 80,000-member miners' union. In August 2007, for example, employer representatives and government officials allegedly colluded to force workers at eight Grupo México mines to break with the SNTMMSRM and join a company-sponsored union.[14]

In March 2006, Gómez Urrutia — with the backing of a number of international union allies — fled into exile in Vancouver, British Columbia.[15] From his base in Canada, Gómez Urrutia and his supporters continued their resistance, both by seeking judicial protection from the government's actions and by organizing a series of costly strikes against Grupo México and other mining-metallurgical enterprises. Government efforts to end a work stoppage

11 ILO, 2008b, points 1262, 1389. In 2008 Gómez Urrutia was re-elected as secretary-general of the union (*La Jornada en línea*, 4 Feb. 2009).

12 The STPS's Associational Registry formally endorsed (Decision no. 21121076, case 10/670-9) the General Vigilance and Justice Council's decision to oust the executive committee led by Gómez Urrutia on the same day that it received notification of the action, even though the Registry's own procedures required it to verify independently the accuracy of the charges. The individual selected by the vigilance council to serve as interim secretary-general, Elías Morales Hernández, had been expelled from the SNTMMSRM in April 2000 for allegedly accepting bribes from Grupo México, although an underlying factor may have been his continuing rivalry with Gómez Urrutia for control of the union (Rendón Corona, 2005, p. 190; Gatica Lara, 2007, p. 76). He was not, however, a union member at the time of his appointment (ILO, 2008b, points 1258, 1292 [f], 1389).

13 ILO, 2008b, point 1291. In September 2007 a Swiss auditing firm contracted by the International Metalworkers' Federation issued a report that found Gómez Urrutia innocent of the charge of embezzling union funds (ibid., point 1292 [j]).

14 ILO, 2008b, points 1346–8, 1401; 'Report', 2009, p. 8.

15 Gómez Urrutia received support from the International Metalworkers' Federation (on whose executive committee he served), the International Federation of Chemical, Energy, Mine, and General Workers' Unions, and the US-based United Steelworkers of America (USWA). On USWA solidarity actions in support of Gómez Urrutia and the SNTMMSRM, see Kay, 2011, pp. 161–3 and a 2010 USWA press release (www.usw.org/media_center/releases_advisories?id=0348).

at the Lázaro Cárdenas, Michoacán steel complex in April 2006 led to the deaths of two workers.[16]

A strike launched in 2007 by workers at the Cananea copper mine in support of Gómez Urrutia and in protest against workplace health and safety violations was on three occasions declared illegal by the Federal Conciliation and Arbitration Board (JFCA), although federal courts suspended each of its rulings (International Labour Organization [ILO], 2008b, points 1356–64). Nevertheless, in February 2010 a federal court finally accepted Grupo México's argument that because of the 'extraordinary conditions' (*fuerza mayor*) produced by the prolonged strike, the existing collective contract must be set aside so that the company could replace striking workers and reopen the mine, which had accounted for some 40 per cent of national copper production. Striking workers enjoyed sufficient support to maintain their occupation of Cananea for several additional months. However, in June 2010 police forces acted without notice and successfully reclaimed the facility.[17] A federal judge subsequently ruled that the police had acted illegally, but the battle for physical control of the mine continued (USLEAP, 2010, p. 3).

The second key event in the mining industry occurred on 19 February 2006. A violent explosion of methane gas at the Pasta de Conchos coal mine in San Juan de las Sabinas, Coahuila killed 65 miners (only two of whose bodies were ever recovered) and injured 11 others (ILO, 2008b, point 1292 [c, d]). The mine, owned by the Grupo México consortium, had repeatedly been cited for workplace health and safety violations — conditions aggravated by subcontracting arrangements condoned by the SNTMMSRM. The accident starkly revealed the inadequacy of workplace-safety enforcement measures in Mexico.

Over the succeeding four years, the miners' families launched more than 50 judicial complaints. Both the National Human Rights Commission (Comisión

16 ILO, 2008b, point 1292 (l). Similar confrontations ended with the death of a SNTMMSRM member in Sonora in 2007 and another in Zacatecas in 2009.

17 *La Jornada*, 7 June 2010, p. 1. According to a paid announcement published by the Mexican Mining Chamber (Cámara Minera de México), the economic cost of the conflict was some US$3.2 billion (Sarmiento, 2010).

The government's action was accompanied by an intensive media campaign highlighting the substantial investments (ostensibly more than US$10 billion) that Grupo México planned to make at Cananea in order to reactivate the local economy and create jobs at the mine. (The company also offered former strikers particularly generous severance packages and promised to rehire the majority of them at a later date.) The sponsors of this campaign — the Private Sector Coordinating Council (Consejo Coordinador Empresarial, CCE), the Mexican Mining Chamber and the National Federation of Independent Unions (Federación Nacional de Sindicatos Independientes), a pro-business, Monterrey-based organization founded in 1936 that by 2010 grouped some 2,400 unions and 230,000 workers — were the principal allies of the government's pro-business labour policy. For paid announcements from these groups supporting the Calderón administration's action, see Chacón, 2010.

Nacional de Derechos Humanos, CNDH) and the International Labour Organization issued reports documenting accumulated violations of workplace safety rules (including 25 violations of ILO conventions, all duly ratified by Mexico, concerning labour administration, occupational health and safety and the use of chemicals) and the responsibility of Grupo México and federal labour authorities for a tragedy that could almost certainly have been avoided simply by installing gas-extraction equipment at Pasta de Conchos.[18] Nevertheless, although four local mine supervisors were convicted of manslaughter, it was not until 2010 that the Court of Administrative and Fiscal Justice (Tribunal de Justicia Fiscal y Administrativa) found the STPS guilty of omission and negligence in the accident, sentencing the ministry to indemnify one victim's surviving family in the amount of approximately US$11,000 (Rodríguez, 2010). It was the first judicial ruling in Mexican history recognizing the legal responsibility of government authorities in a case such as this. If the judgment survives any subsequent appeal, it would open the way for criminal prosecution of those responsible for the Pasta de Conchos tragedy.[19]

The Electrical Workers' Conflict

A protracted conflict involving the Mexican Electricians' Union (SME), the oldest federal-jurisdiction industrial union in the country and an organization with a long history of political independence, further illustrated the grave challenges facing organized labour and the rule of law in Mexico.[20] In October 2009, the Calderón administration once again arbitrarily employed the state's administrative authority in labour matters to challenge the results of a union election. Shortly thereafter, with the union in turmoil and the legal authority of its leaders paralyzed, the government decreed the immediate closure of Central Light and Power (Luz y Fuerza del Centro, LFC), an action that deprived some 42,500 SME members of their jobs at a time when national unemployment was high. The government, however, showed little concern either for labour legality or the social implications of its policies. Instead, its principal motivations were to strike a blow against an independent union that had repeatedly challenged its economic policies, fortify President Calderón's political image at a time when his popularity was declining, and benefit private investors interested in bidding for control of the LFC's optical-fibre network.

18 On the deficiencies of workplace inspections for occupational health and safety risks in Mexico, see Bensusán, 2008.

19 In June 2010, in an action that paralleled the forcible removal of striking workers and the reopening of Grupo México's Cananea mining facility, the Coahuila state government removed from the Pasta de Conchos mine the victims' families who had maintained a vigil at the site in the hope of eventually recovering their relatives' bodies (Muñoz Rios and Ramos, 2010).

20 The SME was founded in December 1914. On the somewhat contradictory internal political dynamics of the union, see Melgoza and Montesinos, 2003, pp. 160–71; Bensusán, 2005b, pp. 546–55.

Central Light and Power's anomalous status and its increasingly fragile financial condition defined the context for these dramatic events. The publicly owned Federal Electrical Commission (Comisión Federal de Electricidad, CFE) became the country's principal power-generation company following the nationalization of the largest private electrical-power firms in 1960, but LFC had survived as an independent company providing electrical power to the Federal District and surrounding states in central Mexico.[21] Nevertheless, because the company depended heavily on government budgetary subsidies, from the mid-1980s onward the SME came under growing pressure to make substantial contract concessions in order to lower LFC's operating costs. As a reward for the SME's political backing for his presidential candidacy in 1988 and because of the government's unwillingness to absorb LFC's outstanding public debt, Carlos Salinas de Gortari had refounded the company by presidential degree in February 1994, thus preserving SME members' jobs and ensuring that they were not forcibly absorbed into the government-allied General Union of Mexican Electrical Workers (Sindicato Único de Trabajadores Electricistas de la República Mexicana). Salinas's action did not, however, address the principal cause of the company's persistent deficits: the regulatory requirement that it purchase electrical power from the CFE at an above-market price that was higher than it was authorized to charge its customers, many of which were public-sector institutions (Chávez Sañudo, 1994, p. 4; Vázquez Trujuque and Vizuet Nava, 2002; *El Universal*, 2009).

Two circumstances — a contested union election and LFC's continuing financial difficulties — provided the Calderón administration with an opportunity to move against the SME. On 9 July 2009, the SME held a highly contested election in which incumbent secretary-general Martín Esparza Flores won re-election by a razor-thin margin of 352 votes out of the 53,368 ballots cast in the election (Muñoz Rios, 2009). The opposition 'Union Transparency' slate challenged the result, and SME treasurer Alejandro Muñoz Resendiz filed a protest with the Federal Conciliation and Arbitration Board charging irregularities in union balloting. In response, the Esparza faction successfully employed a special union assembly on 24 September to remove Muñoz from his post. However, when Esparza then sought STPS acknowledgement of his slate's victory, labour officials ruled on 5 October that the election had been marred by irregularities and refused to certify the election of Esparza and his executive committee.[22] As a result, Esparza lacked legal authority to conduct union affairs.

21 The government established Central Light and Power to operate power-generation facilities previously owned by the Mexican Light and Power Company (Wionczek, 1967, p. 153). In 2009 LFC supplied about one-fifth of the national electrical-power market ('Boletín', 2009).

22 In June 2010 a federal court rejected Esparza's petition for an injunction against the STPS action, thus ratifying the JFCA decision that had nullified Esparza's election (Muñoz Rios, 2010a; Fuentes, 2010).

Acting quickly to exploit this moment of union vulnerability, on 11 October Calderón issued a presidential decree closing LFC with immediate effect, and more than a thousand federal police seized control of all company facilities.[23] Although administration officials argued that this action was legitimate because LFC had been created by presidential decree, many legal experts argued that the government had violated provisions of the Federal Labour Law stipulating that only the JFCA had authority to terminate the collective contract (articles 434, 435) and guaranteeing that a change in employer — in this instance, from LFC to the CFE, which assumed control of all LFC assets — does not affect worker-employer relations in the company or establishment in question (article 41).[24] From the government's perspective, though, the main political advantage of extinguishing LFC by decree was that the SME abruptly lost access to company-deducted union dues and, with them, the resources it needed to contest the government's action.[25]

The Calderón administration immediately launched an aggressive public-relations campaign to justify its actions. The core of its argument was that large-scale government subsidies to LFC (approximately US$3 billion per year) could no longer be justified at a time of national economic hardship, and that the union, whose contract terms allegedly resulted in unreasonably high operating costs, had refused to implement productivity-enhancing reforms essential to restoring the company's economic health. The government published data indicating that public-revenue transfers to LFC (whose operating costs were said to be twice as large as its income) had doubled between 2001 and 2008, and that because of an inflated workforce and rigid contract terms, overall labour costs at LFC represented one-third of the company's total operating expenses, compared to one-fifth at the CFE.[26] What the government failed to mention, however, was that the Federal Accounting Office (Secretaría de

23 Poder Ejecutivo Federal, 2009. The fact that the Fox administration had previously drawn up detailed plans to close LFC may have facilitated the government's action in October 2009 (Middlebrook interview with a former Fox administration labour official, 24 Dec. 2009, Mexico City).

24 See, for example, Alcalde Justiniani, 2009.

25 In July 2010 the Supreme Court concluded that the extinction degree was legal, but it also ruled that the SME remained the legitimate representative of LFC workers. As a consequence, the SME legally regained control over union funds, although full access to them was delayed because STPS authorities refused to recognize the election of Esparza and other members of his executive committee on a timely basis (Brito, 2010; Aranda, 2011a; Bensusán interview with Héctor de la Cueva, Centro de Investigación y Asesoría Sindical, 6 Sept. 2011, Mexico City).

26 Poder Ejecutivo Federal, 2009; 'Boletín', 2009; Malkin, 2009; Hernández, 2007, p. 76. The average salary of a LFC employee in 2009 was approximately 6,600 pesos per month (US$500 at the prevailing exchange rate), roughly four times the minimum wage for the Mexico City area. Contract-provided fringe benefits substantially increased employees' overall income. However, almost 20,000 workers earned less than the LFC average (Muñoz Rios and Martínez, 2009).

Contraloría) had in June 2009 informed LFC management that agreements negotiated with the SME in 2008 to raise productivity, lower labour costs and increase the company's revenue flow, while still protecting workers' jobs, were showing positive results.[27] Nor did it acknowledge that labour contract terms (including retirement benefits, the most costly fringe benefit in the SME's contract) were essentially the same at LFC and the CFE (Bensusán, 2005b, pp. 568–77).

The union countered by arguing that the root of LFC's problems was the government's failure over many years to make the investments necessary to modernize the company's plant and equipment and increase its generating capacity, as well as its obligation to pay more for electricity purchased from the CFE than it could charge its customers. Indeed, the union's 2008–10 productivity agreement with LFC had included commitments to adjust CFE charges and take other steps precisely to address these long-standing problems (Luz y Fuerza del Centro, 2008). However, LFC had a conspicuously poor reputation for customer service, and the general public showed little sympathy for workers who were portrayed (however unfairly) as a 'privileged elite.' Thus, although the SME organized large-scale protests in Mexico City and at other sites in a dozen states, it failed to mobilize much public support.[28] At the same time, the government successfully undercut the SME's leadership by offering highly advantageous terms to workers who were willing to accept severance packages (an average lump sum equal to 33 months' salary), for which a substantial majority of LFC employees opted (*The Economist*, 17 October 2009, p. 67).

The SME's public protests — including hunger strikes in May–July 2010 by a dozen former LFC employees, who acted in the name of approximately 16,500 workers who refused to accept liquidation and struggled to defend their rights — and its legal challenges to the extinction decree continued for many months (Muñoz Rios, 2010b; Martínez, 2010; Notimex, 2011). During this time the Mexico City area endured periodic power outages as the CFE struggled to manage LFC facilities adequately. Nevertheless, the Calderón administration won the battle of public opinion, and with the union no longer able to resist privatization of the optical-fibre network that was once part of

---

27 Martínez and Muñoz Rios, 2009; *El Universal*, 2009; Luz y Fuerza del Centro, 2009. In the 2008–10 productivity agreement, the union agreed to a far-reaching restructuring of workplace relations, on the understanding that workers who were not needed in one production area would be transferred, following appropriate re-training, to areas where they could be productively employed (Luz y Fuerza del Centro/Sindicato Mexicano de Electricistas, 2008 ['Convenio de reestructuración, 2009–2010', clause 3]).

28 For example, the Mexican Union Front (Frente Sindical Mexicano, FSM), which the SME had organized in 1998 primarily as a vehicle for opposing labour law reform, failed to provide significant assistance to the SME in its hour of greatest need. On the origins of the FSM, see Gatica Lara, 2007, p. 77n20.

LFC's holdings, in May 2010 the Ministry of Communications and Transport (Secretaría de Comunicaciones y Transporte) auctioned the network to a consortium led by Televisa, Mexico's largest media company and a leader of the public relations campaign against the SME (Notimex, 2010). In September 2011, government and union negotiators finally reached a settlement that provided for the eventual employment of the LFC employees who had not accepted termination payments. The STPS then immediately certified the 2010–12 re-election of Esparza and his executive committee members (Gómez, 2010b; Muñoz Rios and Martínez, 2011). However, the SME faced a difficult future. The episode demonstrated once again that big business was the ultimate beneficiary of the Calderón government's harsh labour policies.

The Saga of Labour Law Reform

As the SNTMMSRM and SME cases powerfully revealed, labour law provisions granting government officials significant control over the formation of unions, the election of union officers and strikes remained centrally important in state-labour conflicts even after democratic regime change in 2000. Independent unions and their allies in the PRD sought to make labour law reform part of a broader democratization agenda, but it was mainly pressure from business interests that made debates over the content of the 1970 Federal Labour Law a recurring element in Mexican politics from the late 1980s through 2011.[29]

In the view of many private-sector analysts, modifications to labour law that would permit greater flexibility in hiring and working practices and thereby increase labour productivity were one of several 'structural' reforms (along with tax reforms to increase public revenue and constitutional changes permitting private investment in the petroleum industry and in electrical power generation) necessary to ensure Mexico's longer-term economic competitiveness. For example, business interests sought to introduce a greater range of temporary or probationary individual employment contracts; further tighten procedural requirements for strikes and outlaw sympathy strikes; reduce redundancy indemnity payments; sharply constrain seniority (and emphasize occupational training and performance) as a criterion for retention and promotion; and, in general, reduce unions' influence in the workplace and introduce greater flexibility in contract terms and working practices.[30] Government support for private firms' economic restructuring programmes had in fact already introduced considerable flexibility in Mexican labour contracts and working

---

29 See Chapter Three for a discussion of labour law reform efforts between 1987 and 1992. Bensusán, 2000, pp. 408–11, 440–2, De la Garza, 2006b and Zapata, 2006 summarize the various business and union proposals for labour law reform that were formulated from the late 1980s onward. The earliest business proposal was from the Mexican Employers' Confederation (COPARMEX); see Confederación Patronal de la República Mexicana, 1989.

30 De la Garza 2006b, p. 501; Zapata, 2006, pp. 9–10, *passim*; Bizberg, 2003, pp. 235–8.

practices. Nevertheless, some business associations continued to press strongly for legislation that would give these measures the force of law and that would, moreover, raise new obstacles to workers' right to strike.

Business lobbying along these lines gave rise during the mid-1990s to two major proposals for labour law reform that broadly defined the terms of debate over the issue during the following years.[31] In July 1995 the PAN presented an initiative to the federal Senate that promoted greater production flexibility in the workplace by authorizing more frequent use of short-term and probationary contracts, easing terms for laying off employees and making work schedules and terms of compensation more flexible.[32] In an effort to loosen arbitrary union controls and promote constructive dialogue between employers and workers, the draft legislation called for the elimination of exclusion clauses in collective contracts and the creation of employee-elected workplace committees (which were to operate in parallel with union representatives and would have access to information concerning the employer's financial situation) to promote worker participation in company decisions. Moreover, the measure sought to prevent union leaders from abusing the right to strike by requiring the union general assembly to vote in favour of industrial action and by stipulating that, after a strike had been under way for 30 days, either the employer or the union could request compulsory arbitration of the conflict. The bill also transferred responsibility for resolving worker-employer disputes from the executive-controlled, tripartite conciliation and arbitration system to the judicial branch and specially trained 'social judges' (*jueces de lo social*).

Although the PAN's bill focused public attention on a broad range of possible labour law reforms, it also drew criticism from across the political spectrum — from employer groups judging that the proposal was not radical enough, from the CTM and other Labour Congress affiliates fearing the loss of legal prerogatives and bargaining power, and from independent labour organizations concerned that efforts to prevent some union abuses would undercut the workplace position of unions more generally. This debate prompted the Party of the Democratic Revolution to draft its own proposal for labour law reform, a document that accepted some of the PAN's ideas (on, for example, some forms of production flexibility and the transfer of authority over worker-employer disputes to the judiciary), but which primarily sought to democratize state-labour relations and union governance.[33] In particular, the

---

31 See Bensusán, 2000, pp. 410–21, for an examination of labour law reform debates during the 1990s and the context in which they occurred.

32 Partido Acción Nacional, 1995. This discussion draws on Bensusán, 2000, pp. 443–7, table 6.7. In compensation for greater production flexibility, the PAN's proposal offered workers expanded fringe benefits (vacation pay, Christmas bonus, maternity leave) and more favourable terms for worker profit-sharing.

33 Partido de la Revolución Democrática, 1998. Among other proposals, the PRD called for

PRD called for the simplification of union registration procedures, the creation of an autonomous public registry of unions and collective contracts, a secret ballot by rank-and-file members in union elections and in inter-union disputes over representational authority in the workplace, and mandatory rank-and-file access to union statutes and financial statements. The PRD's reform proposals were never formally submitted to the Congress, but they became the basis for the party's draft legislation in 2002 and 2010 (see below).

The PAN and PRD proposals established the parameters of political debate over federal labour law, but continuing business pressures were the principal reason why the Fox and Calderón administrations both attempted to implement broad labour law reform after the PAN won the presidency in 2000. The first effort came in 2001–02, shortly after President Fox took office. In June 2000, just prior to his election, Fox had signed an agreement with independent union leaders ('Twenty Commitments for Union Freedom and Democracy') in which the signatories promised to advance worker rights by democratizing state-labour relations and the labour movement. The document's specific provisions included a public registry of labour organizations and collective bargaining agreements and a requirement that workers vote by secret ballot in union elections and disputes over union representation in the workplace (Alcalde Justiniani et al., 2003, pp. 223–7). These commitments were, however, overturned by the newly inaugurated government's strategic decision to prioritize political and economic stability and seek a de facto alliance with the CTM and other Labour Congress affiliates.

The Labour Congress agreed to participate in controlled negotiations to reform federal labour legislation as part of its dialogue with the Fox administration, but its affiliates were mainly interested in defending the institutional status quo. In essence, CT negotiators were prepared to make substantial concessions on contract terms and working conditions — areas in which employers had long since imposed de facto flexibility — so long as the LFT continued to safeguard the collective rights (in such areas as unionization and collective bargaining) on which their organizational power was based.

In fact, the roundtable discussions convened by the Ministry of Labour and Social Welfare in 2001 did not initially contemplate any profound change in established institutional arrangements. The underlying presumption was that prevailing political conditions — the PAN lacked a majority in the federal Chamber of Deputies — would not permit congressional approval of

a single national minimum wage set by the federal Congress rather than by the executive-controlled, tripartite National Minimum Wage Commission (CNSM); a 40-hour week with 56-hour pay; improved terms for paid vacations, Christmas bonuses and postnatal leaves from work; the elimination of a separate body of labour law (Section B of the Federal Labour Law) for public-sector workers and of state-level labour jurisdiction; and measures to prevent gender and other forms of discrimination in hiring and employment. For an analysis of the PRD proposal, see Bensusán, 2000, pp. 447–50, table 6.7.

constitutional amendments (which would be necessary, for example, to remove from executive control, and give judicial independence to, the conciliation and arbitration board system because it was established by the 1917 Constitution's Article 123). As a consequence, the principal negotiating parties essentially limited themselves to expanding employers' flexibility in the organization of the work process and defending rules that permit officially recognized unions to maintain representational monopolies against workers' will and at the expense of internal union democracy.

Although the National Union of Workers participated in these negotiations primarily to defend its position as the chief rival to the CT, UNT negotiators also sought to advance their goal of democratizing Mexican labour law. Their first priority was to reduce or eliminate arbitrary administrative restrictions on union formation, internal union activities and the right to strike. However, because the leaders of UNT affiliates were more ideologically committed to the principle of union democracy, more accountable to rank-and-file members and more optimistic that grassroots organizing would help them expand their membership than were their CT counterparts, they were also more willing to reduce the various subsidies to union organization embedded in the existing labour law. The UNT's proposals for more far-reaching legal reforms were, nonetheless, systematically rejected in favour of the positions advanced by the Labour Congress and major employer organizations, particularly the Mexican Employers' Confederation (COPARMEX) and the Private Sector Coordinating Council (Consejo Coordinador Empresarial, CCE). When, in October 2002, the UNT and the PRD submitted their own reform initiative to the federal Chamber of Deputies, the government used their action as a pretext to suspend negotiations.[34]

The Calderón administration, working through the PAN's delegation in the Chamber of Deputies, made a second major attempt at labour law reform in March 2010. The terms of the draft legislation were broadly similar to the Fox administration's proposed reform. The draft bill did, however, embrace the International Labour Organization's 'decent work' agenda.[35] It also specifically

---

34 Partido Acción Nacional, 2002; Bensusán, 2003; Bensusán, 2004, p. 281; Bensusán, 2005a, pp. 120–1; Bizberg, 2003, p. 238; De la Garza, 2006b, pp. 502, 509, *passim*; Zapata, 2006, pp. 13–4. The draft reform endorsed by the CT and the CCE (with the support of the PAN, PRI and Mexican Ecologist Green Party [PVEM]) was submitted to the Chamber of Deputies in December 2002. Negotiations within the Chamber and between the legislature and the executive branch continued for nearly three years, but the initiative never came to a final vote, in part because labour organizations of all political stripes voiced opposition to it (Vergara, 2005). For a comparison of the main provisions of this proposal and that submitted by the UNT and the PRD, see Kohout, 2008, table 1 and Mayer, 2003, pp. 82–4.

35 The ILO maintains that countries can achieve the goal of providing 'decent work' by creating jobs, guaranteeing rights at work, expanding social protection and encouraging social dialogue (www.ilo.org/global/about-the-ilo/decent-work-agenda/lang--en/index.htm).

prohibited any form of employment discrimination and substantially strengthened workplace inspection procedures. Moreover, the measure departed from
the Fox administration's proposals by eliminating separation exclusion clauses
in collective contracts, promoting (but not requiring) the use of a secret ballot
in union elections and symbolically strengthening the role of the general
assembly in union governance.[36]

Both the PRD and the PRI rejected the PAN's initiative. The UNT (especially
Francisco Hernández Juárez, leader of the Mexican Telephone Workers' Union
[STRM] and a PRD deputy) then worked through PRD legislators to submit
in April 2010 a separate legislative initiative that paralleled its 2002 reform
proposal.[37] Among other provisions, the bill insisted that workplace flexibility
agreements (including subcontracting arrangements and reductions in working
time) be negotiated through regular employer-union collective bargaining
processes, and it called for the creation of national unemployment insurance.[38]
Like the PAN's proposal, the PRD-UNT measure adopted the ILO's 'decent
work' proposals, prohibited employment discrimination on the basis of gender,
strengthened workplace inspection and removed the separation exclusion clause
in collective contracts, while increasing penalties for employers who engage in
anti-union behaviour.[39]

Most significant, however, the PRD-UNT initiative explicitly sought to
reduce state involvement in union affairs by eliminating government officials'
authority to certify union elections and by creating an autonomous public
registry of unions and collective contracts. The proposed legislation, like the
PAN's 1995 bill and the PRD's 1998 proposal, eliminated the executive-
dominated, tripartite conciliation and arbitration system (as well as state-level
jurisdiction in labour matters) and transferred all responsibility for labour

36 Vergara, 2010; Bensusán, 2011a, pp. 13–5; Partido Acción Nacional, 2010. See Bensusán
    2010a, 2010b and Bouzas Ortiz and Reyes Gaytán, 2010 for critical analyses of the proposal.
        The PAN delegation on the Permanent Commission of the Mexican Congress introduced
    draft legislation in 2009 to reform the Federal Labour Law and the Law on Oversight and
    Accountability (Ley de Fiscalización y Rendición de Cuentas) in order to guarantee union
    members access to information concerning the deduction and use of union dues and the
    contents of collective contracts and union statutes. However, the bill also gave equal
    recognition to secret balloting and public voting in union elections, which would de facto
    continue to protect the position of unaccountable union officials (Garduño, 2009).

37 Bensusán, 2011a, pp. 15–16; Partido de la Revolución Democrática/Unión Nacional de
    Trabajadores, 2010; Bouzas Ortiz and Reyes Gaytán, 2010. The UNT's decision to submit
    a labour law reform proposal that rivalled the PAN's bill aggravated long-standing tensions
    among its affiliates and contributed to the decision by the National Union of Social Security
    Workers (whose leader was then serving as a PAN federal deputy) to secede from the UNT.

38 Unlike Argentina, Brazil, Chile, Uruguay, Ecuador and several other Latin American countries,
    Mexico lacks any form of national unemployment insurance (Velázquez, 2010).

39 The UNT's 2002 labour law reform initiative had also eliminated the separation exclusion
    clause, although the bills it authored in both 2002 and 2010 recognized the validity of
    contracts containing entry exclusion clauses that require employees to join a legally established
    union as a condition of employment.

justice to the federal judiciary. Similarly, it abolished the tripartite National Minimum Wage Commission (CNSM) and transferred authority for setting minimum wages to the federal legislature. Furthermore, it addressed the problem of 'protection contracts' by requiring that collective work agreements be approved by a union's general assembly and by promoting employer-union negotiations at the aggregated level of industrial activity or production chain.[40]

Nevertheless, because neither the PAN nor the PRD controlled a majority of votes in the Chamber of Deputies, neither party's proposal advanced. Thus, the debate remained stalled until March 2011, when members of the PRI's Chamber delegation submitted their own labour law reform proposal. In preceding years the party had proposed modifying specific aspects of labour law, but this was the first occasion since the early 1990s that the PRI had addressed the subject comprehensively. A December 2010 version of the party's proposal largely maintained the state-labour relations status quo, especially where collective union rights were concerned (although it eliminated government officials' authority to certify the election of union executive committees, a surprising departure that the bill's sponsors justified on the grounds that PAN governments had abused this provision of the Federal Labour Law by using it to attack unions).[41] It also substantially improved some benefits for workers (involving, for example, paid vacations and wage premiums for seniority) and reduced the legal working week from 48 to 40 hours. The measure did not, however, adopt the 2010 PAN proposal's language on internal union governance, including the use of a secret ballot in union elections.

Most notably, the initial PRI proposal did not contain the various contract and workplace flexibility measures long advocated by the PAN and leading employer associations. Yet when the draft bill was formally introduced in March, these pro-business measures — including all the PAN's proposals to reduce the cost of worker layoffs, restrict the right to strike and eliminate inter-union conflicts over legal title to contracts — were included.[42] Indeed, the PRI's bill broadly sanctioned outsourcing contracts (establishing that the subcontractor, rather than the final beneficiary of the arrangement, is the legal employer) and permitted apprenticeships and probationary contracts of longer duration than those contemplated by the PAN.[43] The measure also restored

---

40 Bensusán, 2011a, pp. 15–16; Partido de la Revolución Democrática/Unión Nacional de Trabajadores, 2010. Aidt and Tannatos (2002) discuss the advantages that workers derive from collective bargaining systems coordinated at the level of industrial activity. See also Hayter and Weinberg, 2011.

41 Partido Revolucionario Institucional, 2010. Like the other initiatives proposed in 2010–11, the PRI's bill embraced the ILO's 'decent work' agenda.

42 See Partido Revolucionario Institucional, 2011.

43 The PRI's proposal required that outsourcing contracts be written, but they need not be registered with government labour authorities. Nor were they limited to a company's secondary activities, as is typically the case in other countries that regulate outsourcing arrangements.

government officials' authority to certify union elections.[44] These changes were the product of strenuous lobbying by business interests (especially attorneys representing the COPARMEX) and senior Ministry of Labour and Social Welfare officials.[45]

Once the PRI's bill had been modified to reflect employer priorities, the Calderón administration and the PAN's Chamber delegation set aside their own proposal for labour law reform and wholeheartedly embraced the PRI initiative. Their expectation was that a PAN-PRI legislative alliance would permit the government to achieve a long-delayed policy goal. However, a coalition of independent unions, centre-left parties (the PRD, the Labour Party [PT], and Convergence [Convergencia, a small social-democratic party]) and international labour activists mounted a highly vocal campaign against the PRI-PAN proposal.[46] The PRI's own allies in the CTM and the CT also expressed concerns that some of the bill's provisions would weaken the position of unions in the workplace, especially where agreements on production flexibility and outsourcing were concerned. As a consequence, PRI legislators opted to delay action by seeking further public consultations while the measure was debated in committee. The caution shown by PRI legislators was due principally to their fear that a controversial revision of the Federal Labour Law might erode support for their party's candidate in the critically important July 2011 gubernatorial election in the state of México, a contest that was viewed in political circles as an important bellwether in the run-up to the 2012 presidential election.[47]

---

44 Like the PAN's 2010 legislative initiative, the PRI's bill also limited the back wages that a dismissed worker could claim if he or she proved that the firing was without legal justification. The limit proposed by the PRI was more generous (one year's back pay) than that advocated by the PAN (six months' back pay), but the amount was in any event substantially less than the compensation claims typically arising from the lengthy periods workers require to pursue their grievances before conciliation and arbitration boards. See Bensusán, 2007b for an examination of such cases in the garment industry.

45 Statement by Francisco Hernández Juárez at a Chamber of Deputies event on 3 Aug. 2011, Mexico City; Bensusán interviews with a senior Mexican labour lawyer, 3 July and 4 Aug. 2011, Mexico City; Middlebrook interview with a Labour Party (PT) federal deputy, 12 July 2011, London.

The explanatory preface ('exposición de motivos') to the PRI's bill made explicit reference to a much-favoured PAN theme: Mexico's low ranking in international competition indices, particularly with regard to the hiring and dismissal of employees, mandated labour law reform in order to stimulate productivity and economic growth (Partido Revolucionario Institucional, 2011).

46 Méndez and Garduño, 2011a. See also the email messages circulated internationally by the Chicago-based USLEAP (U.S. Labor Education in the Americas Project) on 6 April 2011 and the Toronto, Canada-based Maquila Solidarity Network on 8 April 2011.

In July 2011, Convergence changed its name to Citizen Movement (Movimiento Ciudadano).

47 Alcalde Justiniani, 2011a, 2011b, 2011c; Bensusán, 2011b; Méndez and Garduño, 2011b; Centro de Investigación para el Desarrollo, A.C., 2011a.

The prospects for substantially democratizing the established state-labour relations regime died at the hands of this PAN-PRI legislative alliance. The political odds are that some version of the PAN-PRI measure will eventually be enacted into law. If and when this occurs, the complex interests involved in altering both constitutional provisions and the Federal Labour Law make it highly probable that this action will effectively end debate on the issue for the foreseeable future. It is likely, therefore, that the legal provisions that have long underpinned state-labour relations in Mexico will continue to do so for years to come.

Chapter Five
Shifting Power Resources and the International Defence of Labour Rights in Mexico

The processes of economic liberalization and political democratization radically altered the context in which Mexican labour organizations operated after the early 1980s. Although far-reaching economic restructuring in both the public and private sectors adversely affected 'official' and politically independent unions alike, the economic and political transformations of the 1980s and 1990s posed special challenges for government-allied organizations like those affiliated with the Labour Congress (CT). These unions still drew advantage from the collective-rights provisions in federal labour law that had long underpinned their power in the workplace, and they continued to benefit from their control over labour representation on such tripartite bodies as federal- and state-level conciliation and arbitration boards. As a consequence, the Confederation of Mexican Workers (CTM) and similar groups remained the majority force in the Mexican labour movement and therefore retained some value as strategic allies, trading their capacity to control the demands of rank-and-file union members for overall government support. Nevertheless, with rare exceptions such as the National Education Workers' Union (SNTE), these traditional labour organizations were very much on the defensive. They entered the twenty-first century with smaller memberships, limited bargaining leverage vis-à-vis either employers or government policymakers, reduced political representation in such traditional forums as the federal Chamber of Deputies, and no real capacity to define (and even less ability to implement) a policy agenda addressing the needs of Mexican workers.

The labour organizations best positioned to confront Mexico's new economic and political circumstances were those whose power resources were least dependent on legal subsidies and government support. In particular, unions with greater autonomy vis-à-vis employers and the state, significant organizational and mobilizational capacity, and leaders who derived legitimacy from their accountability to rank-and-file members proved most effective at formulating innovative strategies to address the multiple challenges they faced in the workplace and beyond. The Mexican Telephone Workers' Union (STRM) was, for example, comparatively successful at defending the interests of its members during the 1990 privatization of the Mexican Telephone Company (Teléfonos de México, TELMEX) and mediating the consequences of rapid technological change in the telecommunications industry, though even the STRM struggled to manage such problems as subcontracting arrangements that constrained growth in union membership.[1] Similarly, the National Union of Workers (UNT) was far more willing than its government-allied rivals to accept reforms in federal labour law (especially the elimination of separation exclusion clauses in collective contracts) that would reduce union leaders' coercive authority, increase the power of rank-and-file members in internal union affairs and thereby promote unionization by making membership more attractive.[2]

Politically independent unions were also most actively involved in exploiting the potential offered by international labour rights networks. Although there was certainly no linear relationship between Mexico's changing position in the global economy and the expansion of transnational labour linkages, the country's accession to the North American Free Trade Agreement (NAFTA) in 1994 did have two important consequences in this regard. First, the North American Agreement on Labor Cooperation (NAALC), one of two so-called side agreements negotiated by Canada, Mexico and the United States in conjunction with the NAFTA,[3] created national administrative offices (NAOs) in the three signatory countries to examine allegations of labour rights violations. Although the NAALC's somewhat restricted jurisdiction and the NAOs' limited enforcement capacities have drawn much criticism from labour-rights activists, NAALC grievance processes during the late 1990s did much to raise the international visibility of labour rights issues in Mexico. Moreover, the NAALC framework has served as a focal point for collaborative action by cross-border rights coalitions, which have played an increasingly prominent role in Mexican labour politics. In some instances, NAALC grievance processes have also helped modify Mexican government policies in ways that have benefited workers.

1   Under the terms of its 1989 restructuring agreement with TELMEX, the STRM agreed to link wage increases to improvements in productivity and to accept more flexible work rules. In exchange, the company preserved most union jobs (though the company increasingly hired new workers through non-unionized subsidiaries) and agreed to upgrade workers' skills and award productivity bonuses. A government loan also allowed the STRM to purchase 4.4 per cent of TELMEX stock (Middlebrook, 1995, p. 296; Bensusán, 2004, pp. 267, 270; Clifton, 2000; McLeod, 2004, pp. 164–6, 184).

2   UNT members remain divided over the question of including entrance and separation exclusion clauses in collective contracts.

3   The second agreement was the North American Agreement on Environmental Cooperation.

Second, the intense controversy surrounding the negotiation and approval of the NAFTA contributed centrally to an emerging international debate regarding the appropriate linkage between worker-rights protections and agreements promoting international trade. In this context, the International Labour Organization (ILO), the principal multilateral agency concerned with worker rights and employment issues, has gained new prominence (Hughes and Haworth, 2010). For example, when member states of the World Trade Organization decided in 1998 not to adopt a so-called social charter on labour issues, they noted that it was primarily the responsibility of the ILO to define and advance an international labour-rights agenda (one manifestation of which was the ILO's 1998 'Declaration on Fundamental Principles and Rights at Work'). These developments have encouraged Mexican labour groups to seek ILO support in their efforts to pressure the Mexican government for policy reforms. The ILO's role in this regard parallels the contributions that other multilateral organizations have played in advancing a broader human rights agenda in Mexico.[4]

This chapter examines the rise of North American labour-rights coalitions after the early 1990s and their contributions to the defence of worker rights in Mexico. It particularly focuses on efforts by these coalitions to use grievance petitions filed with the NAALC institutions and the ILO to challenge key elements of Mexico's established state-labour relations regime. The successes have been modest, but these experiences underscore the extent to which the defence of labour rights in contemporary Mexico extends beyond national borders.

The Rise of North American Labour-Rights Coalitions

Mexican workers have formed part of international alliances since the late nineteenth and early twentieth centuries (Carr, 1996, pp. 212–15; Caulfield, 1998, pp. 31–54). In the 1920s, the Mexican Regional Labour Confederation (CROM) developed ties with the US-based American Federation of Labor (Levenstein, 1971), and from the 1950s onward the CTM maintained formal alliances with the American Federation of Labor-Congress of Industrial Organizations (AFL-CIO) and labour movements in other countries via membership in the International Confederation of Free Trade Unions. Especially during the Cold War period, however, these relationships remained quite formulaic. The AFL-CIO's initiatives in Latin America were mainly devoted to containing Communist influence, and the CTM relied on diplomatic formality to safeguard Mexican national sovereignty. As a result,

4   For example, it was a ruling by the Inter-American Court of Human Rights in favour of civilian legal jurisdiction in cases involving human rights violations by the armed forces that led the Mexican Supreme Court to curtail the role that military courts had previously played in this area (Centro de Investigación para el Desarrollo, A.C., 2011b).

their interactions were generally limited to formal exchanges mediated through the Inter-American Regional Workers' Organization.[5]

The political struggle in the early 1990s surrounding the negotiation and approval of the NAFTA produced substantial shifts in the character and intensity of these relationships. The main catalyst for these changes was the growing realization among US and Canadian unionists that the creation of a continental free-trade zone required them to redefine their relationship with Mexican labour organizations in order to defend their own interests. The enactment of the NAFTA called into question the utility of cross-border alliances that were limited to formal expressions of labour solidarity. What was required, they concluded, were democratically-organized partner organizations whose active commitment to raising the wages and improving the working conditions of Mexican workers would in effect help them stem the loss of union members and employment opportunities in their home markets by reducing the economic incentives of Canadian and US firms to move production to Mexico.[6]

The Confederation of Mexican Workers, which had long monopolized the Mexican labour movement's international relations, proved itself an unattractive partner in this regard. The CTM backed President Salinas de Gortari's (1988–94) decision to pursue a free-trade agreement with the United States and Canada, in part because its leaders concluded quite rationally that the foreign direct investment flows stimulated by the agreement would promote job creation (and unionization opportunities) in Mexico. The CTM's only real concern was to restrict as much as possible the labour-rights provisions that Canadian and US unions insisted on attaching to the NAFTA, so that they did not threaten the domestic labour law provisions that underpinned the membership monopolies of its affiliates (Bensusán, 2004, p. 262). In fact, as subsequent events amply demonstrated, Canadian and US challenges to the established position of the CTM and other government-allied unions became the central focus of post-NAFTA labour battles.

For these reasons, then, US and Canadian unions gradually developed ties with Mexican labour organizations less closely aligned with the government

5   Kay, 2011, pp. 39, 41–3. One notable exception to this general pattern was the attempt by the United Automobile, Aerospace, and Agricultural Implement Workers of America (UAW) to build an alliance with Mexican automobile workers' unions in the mid-1960s (Middlebrook, 1982, pp. 142–8).

    Following the fusion of the US-led International Confederation of Free Trade Unions (ICFTU) and the Christian Democratic/Christian Socialist-inspired World Confederation of Labour (WCL) in 2006, the Western Hemisphere branches of the ICFTU and the WCL merged to form the Trade Union Confederation of the Americas, which incorporated the Inter-American Regional Workers' Organization and the Latin American Workers' Central (Central Latinoamericana de Trabajadores) (Collombat, 2011, pp. 7, 10).

6   For a detailed empirical assessment of the actual impact of trade liberalization on labour market conditions in the three NAFTA countries, see Beaulieu, Meza González and Robertson, 2010.

and the ruling Institutional Revolutionary Party (PRI) than the CTM. Some of their most important NAFTA-related contacts were with the Mexican Action Network Against Free Trade (Red Mexicana de Acción frente al Libre Comercio, RMALC), a coalition of labour, environmental and pro-democracy groups founded in April 1991 that led the anti-NAFTA struggle in Mexico.[7] The US-based United Electrical, Radio, and Machine Workers of America (UE) and Communications Workers of America, and the Canada-based Communications, Energy, and Paperworkers Union, were especially active in building alliances in Mexico (Carr, 1996, p. 217; Kay, 2011, pp. 87, 95).

Over time, however, the AFL-CIO also altered its strategies and allegiances, reorganizing its international operations and abandoning its exclusive ties with the CTM. In January 1998, shortly after his election as AFL-CIO president, John Sweeney travelled to Mexico City to inaugurate the American Centre for International Trade Union Solidarity (Centro Americano para la Solidaridad Sindical Internacional), the first such visit by an AFL-CIO president in some 70 years. It was symbolically important that, in addition to meetings with CTM leaders, Sweeney also met with the leadership of the recently formed UNT to discuss how to collaborate more effectively in joint grievance procedures under the NAALC.[8]

More than any other Mexican labour organization, it was the Authentic Labour Front (FAT) that seized upon the opening created by the NAFTA debate to expand its political presence (Bensusán, 2004, p. 269). The FAT, a confederation that in the early 1990s grouped no more than ten thousand workers in small and midsized firms, feared that a continental free-trade agreement and even further market liberalization in Mexico would adversely affect Mexican workers. It became the main force in the RMALC and an active participant in international efforts to embed minimum labour standards in trade and investment agreements. The FAT's commitments to union democracy and international solidarity made it an attractive partner for US and Canadian unions and labour-rights groups, and its international activities increased its political leverage far beyond its direct capacity for social representation. At the same time, its well-established alliance with the UE in the United States and the United Steelworkers in Canada (CUSWA) significantly increased its capacity to undertake unionization drives in the *maquiladora* industry (Carr,

---

7   Information concerning the RMALC's goals and membership is available at www.rmalc.org.mx. See also von Bülow, 2010, pp. 133–40.

8   Bensusán, 2004, p. 258; see also Kay, 2011, pp. 4–5, 72–3, 140. Exchanges between the AFL-CIO and the UNT included information sharing on such topics as the *maquiladora* industry and the unionization of migrant workers, the training of organizers and researchers and other forms of mutual support. In September 1999, the AFL-CIO signed separate cooperation agreements with the CTM, the UNT, the Metropolitan Autonomous University (Universidad Autónoma Metropolitana) and the National Autonomous University of Mexico (Universidad Nacional Autónoma de México) (Bensusán, 2004, p. 258).

1996, p. 217; Kay, 2011, pp. 86–92). It has devoted part of its resources to cadre formation, joint unionization actions with US organizations along the Mexico-US border and protests of labour rights violations filed with the national administrative offices created by the NAALC.

Institutional Focal Points for North American Labour-Rights Coalitions

International actions in support of Mexican workers' rights have focused on a broad range of issues, including freedom of association, workplace health and safety, minimum employment standards and gender discrimination. The most important focal points for these initiatives have been the institutions established by the NAALC and the International Labour Organization. Participation in joint grievance proceedings before these institutions has strengthened cross-border coalitions defending labour rights in Mexico.

The North American Agreement on Labor Cooperation[9]

The North American Agreement on Labor Cooperation was born of the intense political controversy surrounding the NAFTA. The main agreement had been negotiated during 1991–2 by three business-friendly administrations in Canada, Mexico and the United States (those of, respectively, Brian Mulroney, Carlos Salinas de Gortari and George H.W. Bush). However, the measure was not formally ratified before President Bush left office. President Bill Clinton (1993–7; 1997–2001) sought to placate labour allies in the Democratic Party, and make good on his presidential election pledge to promote labour rights and the environment in a North American free-trade area, by negotiating side agreements to the NAFTA in 1993. In these negotiations, US officials confronted considerable resistance from their Canadian and especially their Mexican counterparts, who feared that US demands for intrusive labour-rights protections (and especially trade-based sanctions) constituted a disguised form of protectionism and would violate their national sovereignty (Cameron and Tomlin, 2000, pp. 186–200). For its part, the AFL-CIO offered only tepid support for the labour side agreement (Kay, 2011, pp. 107–9). In the end, the negotiators settled for an agreement that, although creating an important historical precedent by formally linking labour-rights protections to a free-trade agreement, significantly restricted the range of issues subject to trade-based sanctions.

As a consequence, the NAALC distinguishes between two sets of labour rights.[10] The agreement identifies only three areas in which labour law violations can lead to trade-based sanctions: occupational health and safety, child labour

9   This subsection draws on materials in Middlebrook, n.d.

10   The full English-language text of the agreement is available at www.dol.gov/ilab/regs/naalc/naalc.htm.

and minimum wage standards. Nevertheless, the NAALC also includes an appendix (Annex 1) listing 11 broader labour principles that the signatories agreed to promote. These principles include the rights to organize and to strike, the elimination of employment discrimination and the protection of migrant workers.[11] Violations of these rights cannot be punished by trade-based sanctions, but complainants have frequently sought formal investigations of labour law violations in these areas on the grounds that the NAALC's formal statement of objectives obliges the signatories to 'promote, to the maximum extent possible, the labor principles set out in Annex 1' (Article 1[b]). What is at issue in all such cases is whether there is credible evidence that a national government has persistently failed to enforce its own labour laws.[12]

The agencies responsible for investigating alleged labour law violations are the national administrative offices established within the labour or human resources departments of the three signatory countries.[13] Although there are differences in the ways the three NAOs conduct their affairs (for example, whether their investigations into alleged labour rights violations include public hearings), the NAALC requires that a submission on labour law matters be filed in a country other than the one in which the alleged violation occurs (NAALC article 16[3]). Thus, a case alleging labour rights violations in Mexico must be submitted to the Canadian and/or the US NAO. This procedural requirement is in effect an incentive for cross-border cooperation in defence of labour rights within the North American free-trade area, and virtually all the submissions made to NAOs between 1994 and 2010 involved collaboration among trade unions and labour-rights groups in at least two of the NAFTA countries.

The national administrative offices in Canada, Mexico and the United States received a total of 39 public submissions under the NAALC between January 1994 and March 2010.[14] The US NAO received the largest number

---

11 The 11 principles are: freedom of association and protection of the right to organize; the right to bargain collectively; the right to strike; prohibition of forced labour; labour protections for children and young persons; the establishment of minimum employment standards (such as minimum wages and overtime pay) covering wage earners, including those not covered by collective work agreements; elimination of employment discrimination on grounds such as race, religion, age or sex; equal pay for men and women; prevention of occupational injuries and illnesses; compensation in cases of occupational injuries and illnesses; and protection of migrant workers.

12 Grievances cannot, therefore, be filed against private companies or individuals.

13 See NAALC articles 15, 16. The NAALC also established a trinational Commission for Labor Cooperation, which was encharged with promoting cooperative activities among the signatory countries (NAALC articles 8–14).

14 This summary of NAALC submissions is based on data presented in U.S. Department of Labor, 2010. This tally counts the 1997–8 submissions to the US NAO concerning the Han Young plant in Tijuana, Baja California (a submission in October 1997 primarily addressing freedom-of-association issues, and an amendment filed in February 1998 on occupational health and safety matters) as two submissions, on the grounds that the US NAO issued two separate reports on the case.

of filings (24), involving 22 instances of alleged labour-rights violations in Mexico and two in Canada.[15] Trade unions and other labour-rights groups filed nine submissions with the Mexican NAO, all concerning labour-rights issues (freedom of association, minimum labour standards, occupational health and safety) involving Mexican-origin workers in the United States. The Canadian NAO received six submissions, three of which focused on Mexico and three on the US.[16] Most of the submissions (indeed, all of those filed after 1997) alleged violations of more than one NAALC principle. Among the submissions to the US NAO, the allegations in 19 of the 24 cases involved violations of freedom of association and/or the right to bargain collectively; in eight cases, occupational health and safety; in five submissions, minimum employment standards; in five submissions, access to impartial labour tribunals; in three cases, the right to strike; in two cases, the use of child labour; and in one submission, pregnancy-based gender discrimination.

Only the Mexican NAO agreed to review all the submissions it received. The US NAO declined to accept for review six of the cases submitted to it, and the Canadian NAO declined three submissions. In those instances in which a NAO undertook a formal investigation of complainants' allegations, the most common outcome was a recommendation for ministerial consultations between or among the NAFTA governments on the issues involved. The available documentary record does not indicate that the government of the country in which the alleged violation occurred ever declined to engage in such consultations. On at least one occasion, however, a final negotiated settlement was delayed for two years, and the actions undertaken as a result of ministerial exchanges often included activities (public seminars, educational outreach programmes, further consultation and commissioned research) that addressed broad public policy issues but did not necessarily correct labour-rights violations in the company or workplace where the grievance originated. None of the public submissions filed between 1994 and 2010 led to the creation of an evaluation committee of experts (the next step in the NAALC grievance process), and over this period no trade-linked penalties were ever assessed against any of the NAFTA governments for failing to comply with NAALC labour standards.[17]

15 Four of these submissions were withdrawn by the complainants before the review process was completed or public hearings were held.

16 In four instances, complainants filed joint submissions with two national administrative offices (three submissions to the Canadian and US NAOs alleging labour-rights violations in Mexico, and one submission to the Canadian and Mexican NAOs alleging violations in the United States).

17 NAALC articles 21–41 and annex 39 specify the various steps in the grievance resolution process, beginning with ministerial consultations and culminating in the creation of an arbitral panel with the authority to impose monetary sanctions up to an amount equivalent to 0.007 per cent of the total trade in goods between the parties. If the party on which sanctions

A detailed examination of all the NAO filings is beyond the scope of this chapter.[18] However, three of these submissions — the 1997 case regarding gender-discrimination in the Mexican *maquiladora* industry, and the 1997–8 cases involving freedom of association and occupational health and safety at the Han Young auto parts company in Tijuana, Baja California — reveal the strengths and limitations of both transnational labour-rights alliances and the NAALC grievance process. Because this book focuses on labour politics in Mexico, these cases are drawn from the public submissions made to the US National Administrative Office, the most active of the three NAOs where allegations of labour-violations in Mexico were concerned. The gender-discrimination filing was the first NAO case submitted by non-governmental labour-rights organizations without the formal involvement of major trade unions, and it contributed to a significant change in Mexican public policy on workplace discrimination issues. The Han Young cases were among the most controversial of the many US NAO submissions highlighting freedom-of-association problems in Mexico, and they were the first NAO filings to address occupational health and safety issues — one of the three 'tier-one' labour rights endorsed by the NAALC.

The Fight Against Gender Discrimination in the Maquiladora Industry

In May 1997 a coalition of US and Mexican human- and labour-rights groups filed a grievance with the US National Administrative Office (US NAO) alleging discrimination against women workers in the *maquiladora* (export-processing) plants concentrated along the Mexico-US border. Although the gender composition of the *maquiladora* work force has changed over time as male workers have taken an increasing proportion of jobs in these plants, employers in the sector have traditionally recruited young female workers on the assumption that they constitute a more deferential, pliant labour force and are likely to demonstrate greater tolerance for, and physical dexterity in, low-wage assembly tasks.[19] However, hiring young women poses a potential cost risk because Mexico's Federal Labour Law guarantees a 12-week paid maternity leave and other post-maternity benefits. Many *maquiladora* employers have sought to avoid this risk by requiring female job applicants to take a pregnancy test as a condition of employment, or by harassing and intimidating female employees who become pregnant in the hope that they can be forced to resign their position before they give birth.

are imposed does not pay the fine, the other party(ies) may suspend an equivalent amount of NAFTA tariff benefits.

18 For an overview of these cases, see Finbow, 2006 and U.S. Department of Labor, 2010.

19 In 1997 Mexico's National Institute of Statistics, Geography and Informatics (INEGI) reported that 57.7 per cent of production workers in the *maquiladora* industry were women (U.S. National Administrative Office [US NAO], 1998a, item IV (B), note 15). For overviews of the *maquiladora* industry, see Sklair, 1993 and Middlebrook and Zepeda, 2006.

Discriminatory acts of this kind were documented in an investigative report published by Human Rights Watch, a New York-based non-governmental organization (Human Rights Watch, 1996). The author found evidence of widespread gender discrimination in employment practices at 38 of the 43 *maquiladora* firms studied in five northern cities (Tijuana, Baja California; Chihuahua, Chihuahua; and Matamoros, Reynosa and Rio Bravo, Tamaulipas), where prospective female employees were required to take pregnancy tests or answer intrusive questions to determine whether they were, or were likely to become, pregnant. Pregnant applicants were routinely denied employment, and women who became pregnant after they were hired were often verbally abused, given difficult job assignments or less favourable work shifts, or otherwise harassed by supervisors in concerted efforts to provoke their resignation. As a consequence, female employees concealed their pregnancies and accepted unsafe work assignments (involving, for example, exposure to industrial chemicals or other hazardous materials) in order to avoid dismissal. Women workers felt unable to challenge these practices for fear of being blacklisted and denied future employment in the *maquiladora* sector.[20]

The public submission that Human Rights Watch (Human Rights Watch Women's Rights Project and Human Rights Watch/Americas) made to the US NAO on 16 May 1997 was based on this report.[21] It was seconded by another US non-governmental organization (NGO), the Washington, DC-based International Labor Rights Fund, and the Mexico-based National Association of Democratic Lawyers (Asociación Nacional de Abogados Democráticos, ANAD).[22] As required by the terms of the NAALC, the complainants charged that the Mexican government had failed to enforce effectively its own laws (NAALC article 3[1]) prohibiting gender discrimination and to provide adequate access to administrative, quasi-judicial or labour tribunals to enforce the law (NAALC article 4 [1, 2]). The groups making the submission noted that the NAALC's list of labour principles (Annex 1) specifically bars discrimination on the basis of race, religion, age, sex or other grounds. Moreover, they argued that gender discrimination in hiring and employment violates the ILO's convention 111 ('Discrimination in Respect of Employment and Occupation'), the United Nations' International Covenant on Civil and Political Rights and its Convention on the Elimination of All Forms of Discrimination Against Women (CEDAW), and the American Convention on Human Rights — all of which had been ratified by Mexico.

---

20 In cities with high concentrations of *maquiladora* plants, companies often maintain blacklists of union organizers and other individuals whom they wish to bar from employment.

21 This discussion draws on documents included in US NAO, 1998a.

22 In 1996 these three groups had collaborated in submitting a complaint to the US NAO (US NAO submission 9601) concerning freedom of association for Mexican federal employees.

The US NAO agreed on 14 July 1997 to investigate the case (designated US NAO 9701), and on 19 November 1997 it held a public hearing in Brownsville, Texas on the issues in dispute. Witnesses at the hearing included both experts on Mexican labour law and employer practices and five women workers employed in *maquiladora* plants. Two elements made this a notable case: it was the first case the US office had considered that did not allege violations of freedom of association and/or collective bargaining rights, and it was brought by human- and labour-rights NGOs rather than by trade unions.[23]

In its responses to the US NAO, Mexico's National Administrative Office denied that pregnancy testing in the *maquiladora* industry was as widespread as Human Rights Watch alleged. The main point of controversy, however, concerned the legality of pre-employment pregnancy testing. Mexican officials argued that national labour law did not expressly prohibit screening of this kind and that it was impossible for anyone to pursue a claim for gender discrimination prior to the existence of a formal employment relationship (US NAO, 1998a, item III[D]). Nor, under these circumstances, could institutions such as conciliation and arbitration boards be faulted for failing to enforce the law adequately. The US NAO had, then, exceeded the scope of its mandate under the terms of the NAALC.

The US NAO issued findings and recommendations on 12 January 1998 that broadly endorsed the complainants' charges. It reaffirmed that post-hire discrimination against pregnant women is clearly illegal under Mexican law, while acknowledging differing views among Mexican officials (and some ambiguity in ILO convention 111 and the CEDAW) concerning the legal status of pre-employment pregnancy screening. Nevertheless, the US NAO argued that under the terms of the NAALC the matter was an appropriate subject of ministerial consultations between the United States and Mexico (US NAO, 1998a, item VII). It based this conclusion in part on evidence it received that senior Mexican labour officials had themselves sought the voluntary cooperation of *maquiladora* employers to end a practice that they considered inappropriate, even if technically legal (US NAO, 1998a, item VI). The US NAO found particularly damning an analysis of women's issues prepared by Mexico's Ministry of the Interior (Secretaría de Gobernación) that stated

> To some extent the practices of dismissal for reason of pregnancy and the requirement of non-pregnancy certification to obtain employment persist ... Additionally, women workers are frequently subjected to discriminatory practices in obtaining employment and in dismissal from employment for reason of pregnancy or because they are nursing.[24]

23 Kay (2011, table 4.3) indicates that the FAT was involved in this case, but there is no evidence of this in the documents related to US NAO 9701.

24 Secretaría de Gobernación, *Alianza para la Igualdad: Programa Nacional de la Mujer, 1995–*

Javier Bonilla, Mexico's minister of labour and social welfare, responded to a formal request from his US counterpart by agreeing to consultations on the matter, and the two labour ministries subsequently announced a series of cooperative activities designed to counter gender discrimination in the workplace and raise public awareness of the problem (Finbow, 2006, p. 95). These actions did not, however, address the issue of pre-hire discrimination because the Mexican government insisted that this would in effect constitute an expansion of labour rights and exceed the NAALC's mandate to focus on the enforcement of existing national laws.

Nevertheless, by increasing public awareness of the issue, the NAO proceedings did contribute to policy change in Mexico. At a trinational conference convened in March 1999 to examine pregnancy-based discrimination in the workplace and gender discrimination in the three NAFTA countries, Mexican labour officials publicly acknowledged for the first time that employment discrimination on the basis of gender and pregnancy (both pre- and post-hire) is illegal under Mexican law (U.S. Department of Labor, 2010). Furthermore, they announced the creation of a new women's bureau at the Ministry of Labour and Social Welfare (STPS) and an educational outreach programme for women in the *maquiladora* industry (Finbow, 2006, p. 95). There was no amendment of the Federal Labour Law specifically to ban pre-hire pregnancy screening, but in October 1999 Rosario Robles, the first female governor of the Federal District, amended the district's penal code to bar pregnancy-based discrimination. The Ministry of Public Education (Secretaría de Educación Pública) also ended pregnancy tests as a condition of employment, and in 2003 Mexico adopted a broad anti-discrimination law that explicitly prohibited gender- or pregnancy-based discrimination in hiring.[25] The resonance of the NAO proceedings may have been amplified in this instance by the fact that there was already an awareness of the issue in Mexican policymaking circles and an emerging commitment to address the problem of pregnancy-based discrimination.[26]

2000 (March 1996), pp. 88–90, cited in US NAO, 1998a, item IV(E) (translation by US NAO staff) and item VI. A 1995 report by the Human Rights Commission of the Federal District similarly found evidence of pre-employment pregnancy testing in several federal agencies located in the Federal District, practices which it judged unconstitutional (US NAO, 1998a, items IV[F], VI).

25 Williams, 2005, pp. 145–6. See also the 'Decreto por el que se expide la Ley Federal para Prevenir y Eliminar la Discriminación', *Diario Oficial de la Federación*, 11 June 2003 (www.dof.gob.mx).

26 There are also indications that some *maquiladora* firms, especially the subsidiaries of major US corporations, changed their employment policies as a result of the negative publicity generated by the Human Rights Watch report and the US NAO case (Human Rights Watch, 1998, appendices B, C, E, G, J). Nevertheless, there was evidence of pre-employment pregnancy screening at a *maquiladora* plant in the state of Hidalgo as late as July 2005 (US NAO, 2007, item 8).

The Struggle for Freedom of Association at Han Young

No less than 17 of the 22 public submissions filed with the US NAO between 1994 and 2010 alleged violations of Mexican workers' right to freedom of association. Indeed, before the submission on gender discrimination in May 1997 (US NAO 9701), **all** of the US NAO filings had addressed this issue as US unions and their Mexican allies used the NAALC grievance process to challenge the established state-labour relations regime in Mexico. These efforts focused particularly on unionization efforts in the *maquiladora* industry, a sector whose growth was largely fuelled by US manufacturing companies moving production (and jobs) to Mexico and in which politically independent, representative trade unions were virtually non-existent.[27] The Han Young case therefore formed part of a much broader, concerted effort by Mexican and US labour groups to promote independent union organizing in the maquiladora industry. The case was nevertheless notable both for the range of Mexican and US trade unions and labour-rights groups involved and for the exceptionally high level of political attention it received.

The conflict began in April 1997 when a group of workers at Han Young de México, a Korean-owned company employing approximately 120 people in the assembly of truck chassis for Hyundai Precision America (a subsidiary of Hyundai Corporation) in Tijuana, Baja California, sought to organize an independent union.[28] They acted out of mounting discontent with their existing union, an affiliate of the Revolutionary Confederation of Workers and Peasants (CROC, one of Mexico's major government-allied labour confederations) that had failed to secure improved wages and working conditions or to address serious workplace health and safety problems. Although workers at the plant were regularly exposed to airborne toxic contaminants as a result of welding and other manufacturing processes, there was insufficient exhaust ventilation, exposure monitoring, health and safety training or other hazard-control measures. Nor did the company provide workers with adequate protective equipment, such as safety shoes and glasses, respirators, face shields and chemical-resistant gloves.

On 2 June 1997 the dissident Han Young employees conducted a one-day work stoppage in support of their demands, but they suspended the action the next day when company managers evidenced some willingness to address their concerns. Two weeks later, Baja California state labour inspectors responded positively to a petition from the workers and conducted a health-and-safety inspection of the plant, after which they notified the company that

---

27 US NAO, 1998b, item V(C2); Bandy, 2005. These sources identify only three independent unions in the entire *maquiladora* sector between the early 1980s and late 1990s, even though in December 1997 the sector's 2,867 firms employed 938,438 workers.

28 This discussion draws on US NAO, 1998b, especially items II(A), V(A); 1998c, items II(A), VI.

it would have to rectify some two dozen deficiencies (including inadequate ventilation, electrical hazards, unsafe materials handling and lack of personal protective equipment for workers) within 25 working days at most.[29] However, workplace relations worsened in mid-July when the company's new director of human resources began a systematic campaign of harassment against the protest organizers. Some workers (including the three union representatives on the newly created employer-worker health and safety committee) were fired, and the company offered them severance payments in an unsuccessful effort to dissuade them from filing reinstatement claims with the state-level Local Conciliation and Arbitration Board (Junta Local de Conciliación y Arbitraje, JLCA).

At about this time the Han Young employees suspended their independent unionization efforts and agreed to affiliate themselves with the FAT's Union of Workers in the Metal, Iron, Steel and Related and Similar Industries (Sindicato de Trabajadores en la Industria Metálica, Acero, Hierro, Conexos y Similares, STIMAHCS). On 6 August, the STIMAHCS formally petitioned the JLCA to replace the CROC's José María Larroque Union of Workers in Various Occupations (Unión de Trabajadores de Oficios Varios 'José María Larroque') as the legally recognized collective bargaining representative at Han Young. Company managers responded by bringing in some 20 new employees in an attempt to dilute workforce support for the STIMAHCS, and CTM representatives visited the plant in an effort to win workers' support and prevent the STIMAHCS from consolidating its position. Nevertheless, the JLCA proceeded to schedule a recount election on 6 October to determine which union — the CROC affiliate or the STIMAHCS — enjoyed majority worker support.[30]

Despite substantial irregularities in the representation election, the STIMAHCS won the vote by a margin of 54–34. However, company managers continued to fire union supporters and hire non-union replacement workers. Then, on 10 November, the JLCA declared that the STIMAHCS was ineligible to represent Han Young workers (on the grounds that it was registered as a national union in the metallurgical sector, rather than in the automotive sector), annulled the results of the recount election and ruled that the CROC retained legal control over the collective contract.

On 30 October, as the labour conflict at Han Young escalated and gained

29 In a follow-up visit to the plant on 5 September, labour inspectors found that Han Young had corrected 18 of the 23 health-and-safety deficiencies they had identified in June. They decided against levying fines or other sanctions at that time, although they did levy fines equivalent to US$9,400 on 28 November when they determined that some deficiencies continued to exist. Baja California officials conducted three further inspections of the plant in January and March 1998, finding that some serious workplace hazards had still not been corrected. US NAO, 1998c, item VI.

30 The CTM withdrew from the contest on the day of the representation election.

increasing international notoriety, a coalition of four US and Mexican labour-rights groups filed a public submission with the US NAO alleging systematic violations of Han Young workers' right to choose which union would represent them and the Mexican government's failure to ensure the fairness and impartiality of its labour tribunals. The complainants were the San Diego, California-based Support Committee for Maquiladora Workers (SCMW, whose director had been involved from the outset in efforts to organize an independent union at Han Young), the STIMAHCS, the International Labor Rights Fund and the National Association of Democratic Lawyers.[31] The Berkeley, California-based Maquiladora Health and Safety Support Network formally joined the case in December 1997, and in February 1998 it filed a supplemental submission alleging serious occupational health and safety problems at the Han Young plant. This action was endorsed by Worksafe! Southern California and three of the most powerful Canadian and US labour organizations: the Canadian Auto Workers, the United Automobile, Aerospace, and Agricultural Implement Workers of America (UAW) and the United Steelworkers of America (USWA), all of which joined the case as co-submitters.[32] The US NAO formally accepted the submission (designated US NAO 9702) for review on 17 November.

Even as the US NAO proceedings began, the Mexican federal government intervened in an effort to mediate the Han Young conflict. Federal and state officials together reached an agreement with workers and management that included convening a new representation election, which was held on 16 December. Company managers offered pay-offs to workers willing to vote in favour of CTM representation, but the STIMAHCS again prevailed by a narrow margin. On 12 January 1998 the JLCA granted registration to the independent 'October 6' Union of Industrial and Commercial Workers (Sindicato de Trabajadores de la Industria y del Comercio '6 de octubre') and recognized it as the legal bargaining representative at the plant.[33] All but one of the workers who had been dismissed for union organizing activities accepted reinstatement. Nevertheless, in subsequent months company managers continued to harass and sometimes dismiss union activists, hired non-union replacement workers in an attempt to undercut the new union, and conspired with the CROC and the CTM to convene yet a third union representation election that might return control over the plant's collective contract to a more pliant labour organization (US NAO 1998b, items II[A], V[A]).

31 On the SCMW's involvement at Han Young, see Williams, 2003.

32 Kay (2011, p. 140) reports that the AFL-CIO also offered behind-the-scenes support for the Han Young workers.

33 In the second representation election, a total of 30 Han Young workers voted for the STIMAHCS, 26 for a CTM affiliate and two for the CROC (US NAO, 1998b, item II[A]). The Tijuana press reported that the CROC's national secretary-general accepted a substantial pay-off in exchange for deferring to the CTM in the case (Williams, 2003, p. 536).

On 18 February 1998 the US NAO held a public hearing on the case in San Diego, at which it heard testimony from the complainant organizations, Han Young workers and employer representatives, and expert witnesses called to testify about union organizing conditions in the *maquiladora* industry. Han Young's owner and managers summarily denied the allegations made against them. They claimed that they were not opposed to any union, whatever its organizational affiliation, so long as it clearly enjoyed majority worker support. Moreover, they denied that anyone had been fired for union organizing activities; employees who had been dismissed either had failed to perform their jobs satisfactorily or had violated company policies. Han Young managers also asserted that health and safety conditions were perfectly adequate, noting that the plant had been subject to frequent state inspections (US NAO 1998b, III[C], V[a]; 1998c, III[C]).

The US NAO issued two reports on the Han Young conflict, the first on freedom-of-association issues (28 April 1998) and the second on occupational health and safety questions (11 August 1998). The reports dismissed several of the complainants' allegations (concerning, for example, some employment practices at the Han Young plant), but on balance the US NAO found that their claims had merit. Officials from the US NAO were not persuaded by the employer's testimony in the case, although they recognized that Hyundai Precision America had played a positive role by pressuring Han Young managers to correct serious workplace health and safety problems and resolve the conflict. They expressed serious doubts about the impartiality of the JLCA at different junctures, and they were also troubled by the JLCA's unexplained decisions in November 1997 to reverse itself on the question of STIMAHCS eligibility to represent Han Young workers and to annul the 6 October election. Moreover, the US NAO report on occupational health and safety issues noted that, although plant inspections had been thorough and consistent with Mexican laws and regulations, it was unclear whether Han Young had ever paid the various fines levied against it for workplace health and safety violations (US NAO 1998b, items III[C], V[A, B1], VI; 1998c, III[C], VII).

The US NAO did, however, acknowledge that the JLCA's conduct in September and October 1997 was on the whole appropriate and reasonable, and it applauded both the Mexican federal government's efforts to resolve the Han Young conflict and on-going federal programmes designed to improve the functioning of conciliation and arbitration boards (including the consistency with which they applied juridical criteria). It also recognized that, although some health and safety problems still existed at the plant, the negative publicity generated by the case and pressures from federal labour authorities had led to significant improvements in workplace conditions at Han Young (US NAO, 1998b, items V[B1, C2], VI; 1998c, items VI, VII). Yet, despite these findings, the US NAO went on to recommend binational ministerial consultations on Mexico's provisions for union representation elections, the conduct of conciliation and arbitration boards, and ways of improving the effectiveness and deterrent effect of workplace inspections (US NAO 1998b, item VI; 1998c, item VII).

This conclusion drew a sharp rebuttal from STPS representatives, who stated that the US NAO was 'supporting the demands of one side in this dispute, stirring up emotions and generating hopes that go beyond the terms of the North American Free Trade Agreement' (Dillon, 1998). Javier Bonilla, the STPS minister, may have acquiesced to consultations with US Secretary of Labor Alexis Herman as early as October 1998 (Finbow, 2006, p. 100), but a formal agreement concerning the Mexican government's response was delayed until 18 May 2000. At that time the U.S. Department of Labor and Mexico's Ministry of Labour and Social Welfare issued a joint report on the first Han Young submission and on another controversial freedom-of-association case in which they, 'in a spirit of cooperation and complete respect for the sovereignty of each country regarding labor law and practice on the principles of freedom of association and protection of the right to organize', addressed the main issues raised by these submissions.[34] The report was especially significant because Mexican labour authorities agreed for the first time that secret ballot procedures would be employed in future votes to resolve conflicts over title to collective contracts. They also agreed to combat 'employer protection contracts' by promoting access to information concerning collective work agreements, thereby supplementing an STPS website displaying information regarding all registered unions.[35]

An extensive solidarity movement in the United States and Canada mobilized behind the Han Young workers' demands. International observers had been present at the 6 October union representation election, and in

---

34 U.S. National Administrative Office, 2000 ('Joint Declaration'). The second case (filed on 15 December 1997 and designated US NAO 9703) alleged violations of freedom of association and workplace health and safety rights at ITAPSA, a subsidiary of the US-owned Echlin Corporation manufacturing parts for auto brake systems in the state of México.

35 These lists are available at http://registrodeasociaciones.stps.gob.mx/regaso/ consultaregasociaciones.asp and http://contratoscolectivos.stps.gob.mx/RegAso/legal_ contratos.asp. The Mexican government's commitment to disseminate union registration information via the Internet apparently dated from the STPS's 'Programme for Employment, Training and Defence of Labour Rights, 1995–2000.' See U.S. National Administrative Office, 2000.

The 18 May 2000 joint agreement on the Han Young and ITAPSA/Echlin cases also included a commitment to hold public seminars in Tijuana and the Mexico City area on freedom-of-information issues. The Tijuana seminar was convened in June 2000, but it quickly ended in violence. The meeting was disrupted by two dozen protesting Han Young workers carrying banners demanding workplace justice, who were physically attacked by CROC affiliates in the audience. These events unfolded in front of STPS Undersecretary Javier Moctezuma Barragán and US NAO Secretary Lewis Karesh (Bacon, 2000).

November 1997 the Han Young union's Canadian and US allies conducted a one-day fast in solidarity with four Han Young workers who had gone on hunger strike to pressure the Baja California conciliation and arbitration board to recognize the 6 October election victory (Kay, 2011, p. 136). Solidarity protests targeted Hyundai automobile dealerships in a number of US cities in early 1998, and from July through September 1998 trade unions and labour-rights activists organized similar actions throughout the United States and Canada, culminating in a 'Han Young Action Day' on 19 September.[36]

The Han Young case attained such prominence in part because it coincided with an intense political battle in the United States over presidential authority to negotiate free-trade agreements like the NAFTA. The US Trade Act of 1974 required periodic congressional renewal of the executive branch's authority to negotiate trade agreements on a 'fast-track' basis (meaning that the Congress can approve or disapprove of proposed trade pacts but cannot amend or filibuster them). Many congressional Democrats opposed renewing 'fast-track' authority in 1997–8 unless the legislation required US trade negotiators to include strong environmental and labour-rights safeguards in any future trade agreements. In their fight against 'fast-track' legislation, several congressmen with close ties to the US labour movement (including Richard Gephardt, the Democratic majority leader in the House of Representatives and an aspirant to the Democratic presidential nomination in 2000, and David Bonior, the Democratic majority whip in the House) cited the Han Young case as an example of the NAALC's failure to protect worker rights (O'Connor, 1997; Kay, 2011, p. 138). Vice President Albert Gore, acting at the behest of senior Democratic congressional leaders, discussed the Han Young case directly with Mexican President Ernesto Zedillo (1994–2000) during Zedillo's visit to Washington, DC in November 1997 in an effort to assuage congressional criticism (Williams, 2003, p. 534; Kay, 2011, p. 137).

The political pressures generated by the international Han Young coalition no doubt had a significant impact on the US NAO's commitment to the case and the Mexican federal government's efforts to resolve the conflict. However, despite the international support they received in their protracted struggle for a politically independent, representative union and improved wages and working conditions, Han Young workers found it impossible to defend their hard-won gains in the workplace. Other *maquiladora* employers and Baja California state government officials, fearing the precedent of an independent union and its possible impact on the local investment climate, urged Han Young's owner not to negotiate with the new union. In March 1998, even before the US NAO issued its first report on the case, the company announced it would relocate its

---

36 Williams, 2003, pp. 542–3; Kay, 2011, pp. 136–7. Williams (2003, p. 548n9) provides an extensive list of the solidarity events organized in support of Han Young workers.

plant to another part of Tijuana and began to lay off workers (Williams, 2003, p. 538–9).

In an effort to defend their movement and their jobs, in late May 1998 Han Young workers manoeuvred to freeze company assets by declaring a strike before the factory closed. However, the night before their planned action, CTM enforcers occupied the plant in order to keep it open (Bacon, 1998; Williams, 2003, p. 540). The state-level conciliation and arbitration board subsequently claimed that the CTM had won a new union representation election and declared the Han Young workers' strike action illegal on a technicality (Bandy, 2005, p. 314). A federal court judge in Mexicali, the state capital, issued three separate injunctions against the bogus representation election and ordered the JLCA to respect Han Young workers' right to strike (Bacon, 2000). Nevertheless, the Tijuana police blocked Han Young employees' attempts to regain control of their workplace, and their efforts to shut down the new manufacturing site in eastern Tijuana were unsuccessful (Williams, 2003, p. 543). The struggle continued through at least July 2000, but it eventually failed (Kay, 2011, p. 138).

The International Labour Organization

International institutional action in defence of Mexican workers' rights did not begin with the NAFTA and the NAALC. The International Labour Organization remains the principal multilateral agency responsible for the promulgation of international labour standards, and Mexican unions have frequently had recourse to ILO grievance procedures. For example, between 1954 and 2010 they filed 48 complaints (43 of which had been concluded by 2010) with the ILO's Committee on Freedom of Association alleging that the Mexican government was not abiding by the terms of ILO convention 87 on 'Freedom of Association and Protection of the Right to Organise.'[37] The Committee has the authority to investigate such complaints and issue reports of its findings, but it has no enforcement powers other than the ILO's capacity for moral suasion.[38]

---

37 ILO, 2011, item 883. Mexico has ratified ILO convention 87 (1948) but not convention 98 (1949) on 'Right to Organise and Collective Bargaining', apparently on the grounds that it conflicts with the contract-based entrance and separation exclusion clauses allowed by the Federal Labour Law (ILO, 2011, item 790). However, the ILO notes (2006, items 363–4) that union security clauses that are permitted (but not mandated) by national law are not contrary to the principle of freedom of association and are left to the discretion of ratifying states.

On the more general problem of Mexico's compliance with the ILO's fundamental labour standards, see Bensusán, 2009, table 2, pp. 24–5.

38 Hughes and Haworth, 2010, pp. 27–9. See ILO, 2006, Annex 1 for ILO procedures in the examination of complaints alleging violations of freedom of association.

Many of the recent Mexican petitions to the ILO have focused on the proliferation of 'employer protection contracts.' This phenomenon reflects deep-rooted complicity among employers, unaccountable or spurious union leaders and government officials. For many years these contracts were largely restricted to smaller firms in the construction and garment industries. Since the 1980s, however, they have become ubiquitous in some of the country's most dynamic economic activities (including the auto parts industry, banks, commercial aviation, franchises of all kinds and, especially, *maquiladora* plants) as company lawyers increasingly rely on such agreements to establish unilaterally the terms of employment (Bensusán, 2007a; Bouzas Ortiz and Reyes Ramos, 2007). Once in place, the force of law protects the employer from efforts by an authentic union to improve workers' wages, fringe benefits or working conditions.

In 2007, a broad coalition of national and international unions and labour-rights groups initiated a high-profile campaign against the practice, culminating in a complaint that the International Metalworkers' Federation (IMF) filed with the ILO's Committee on Freedom of Association in 2009.[39] The petition was endorsed by the International Trade Union Confederation and three Mexican unions, the Independent Union of Metropolitan Autonomous University Workers (Sindicato Independiente de Trabajadores de la Universidad Autónoma Metropolitana), the Union of Workers in the Metal, Iron, Steel and Related and Similar Industries (STIMAHCS), and the Mexican Mining and Metalworkers' Union (SNTMMSRM).[40] Both the STIMAHCS, an affiliate of the FAT, and the SNTMMSRM had considerable experience in transnational labour alliances.

Over the next two years the ILO's Committee on Freedom of Association reviewed extensive written testimony from the IMF and other sources concerning the myriad bureaucratic hurdles and administrative delays that workers frequently face in their efforts to exercise their legal right to association, including requests for documentation by labour authorities that expose prospective union members to sanction or dismissal by their employer.[41] It also

39 For the roster of organizations participating in the campaign against employer protection contracts, see Blanke, González and Hernández, 2008, p. 3.

40 The materials cited in this section are drawn from ILO, 2011. The IMF's complaint was filed on 5 February 2009. The Government of Mexico challenged the admissibility of the complaint and made observations on the complainant's allegations on 1 March 2010.

41 The IMF's petition detailed three prominent cases over the 2003–10 period in which government authorities denied or seriously delayed union registration: the National Union of Petroleum Technicians and Professionals (Unión Nacional de Técnicos y Profesionistas Petroleros); the Commercial, Office, Retail and Similar and Allied Workers' Union of the Federal District (Sindicato de Trabajadores de Casas Comerciales, Oficinas y Expendios, Similares y Conexos del Distrito Federal); and the Johnson Controls union. For details, see ILO, 2011, items 797, 798 and 799, respectively.

heard evidence that the certification of union elections is a highly discretionary process. Most important, it documented (including testimony from trade union leaders and corporate attorneys) the high frequency with which employers seek out compliant union leaders in order to negotiate — almost always without the knowledge or participation of the workers affected — protection contracts that limit employees' rights to the minimum requirements specified by the Federal Labour Law.[42] Once in place, these contracts have the force of law and, as a practical matter, make it virtually impossible for workers to choose another union representative because conciliation and arbitration boards typically reject (on the grounds that it would disrupt 'social peace') petitions to hold a special election to determine which labour organization has majority worker support (ILO, 2011, items 732–5, 737–8).[43]

The Ministry of Labour and Social Welfare filed a detailed rebuttal of the IMF's accusations that included supporting testimony from several Mexican labour confederations and employer associations.[44] The ministry flatly denied the IMF's charges: '... the Mexican Government has never infringed the right of association by any Mexican worker' (ILO, 2011, item 846); '... the Government of Mexico does not violate, or limit at any time, either the fact or right of freedom of association or collective bargaining of workers' (ibid., item 875). Moreover, it both emphasized the protective content of federal labour law and noted the existence of legal recourse if workers' rights are violated (ibid., items 816, 837, 883). In essence, the STPS argued that violations of ILO convention 87 on freedom of association do not occur in Mexico because it is logically impossible for them to occur ('Thus, in no way can it be argued that the Mexican Government violates the labour laws which the Government itself promotes and supports'; ibid., item 816). It took a similarly Kafkaesque position on the issue of protection contracts: 'The Mexican judicial system does not contemplate the concept of so-called employer protection contracts, and for this reason the Mexican government does not in any way recognize the existence of such contracts.'[45]

---

42 Because collective work agreements can be terminated by mutual agreement of the signatory parties, employers who have signed protection contracts with unaccountable or corrupt union leaders can easily lower their labour costs by terminating the agreement and then rehiring workers at lower wage rates (ILO, 2011, item 745).

43 Indeed, the Ministry of Labour and Social Welfare has apparently encouraged leaders of major trade union confederations to sign 'agreements on respect and collaboration' in which they promise not to challenge each other's established title to collective contracts (ILO, 2011, item 738).

44 These groups included the Confederation of Mexican Workers (CTM), the Revolutionary Confederation of Workers and Peasants (CROC), the Mexican Employers' Confederation (COPARMEX) and the National Confederation of Chambers of Industry (Confederación Nacional de Cámaras Industriales). Their principal observations appear in ILO, 2011, items 837, 852, 855, 858–61, 867, 869–70, 874, 885.

45 Secretaría del Trabajo y Previsión Social, 2010, p. 29; ILO, 2011, items 875–6, 879. The STPS

In its final report on the IMF's complaint (issued on 11 March 2011), the ILO panel noted that this was not the first occasion on which it had received allegations of violations of the right of association in Mexico:

> The Committee wishes to point out that on previous occasions it has requested certain legislative reforms to strengthen trade union rights, and has found that there has been excessive delay by the administrative or judicial authorities in relation to the registration of certain trade unions or the recognition of certain trade union executive boards; in addition, the Committee has been made aware of cases of violence between trade union factions which claimed to be more representative (ILO, 2011, item 899).

For the most part, though, the Committee on Freedom of Association limited its recommendations to calling on the Mexican government to initiate a constructive dialogue with workers' organizations (including the complainants) and employers' associations concerning protection contracts, exclusion clauses, the minimum representativeness of trade unions engaged in collective bargaining, and the impartiality of conciliation and arbitration boards and the length of their proceedings. However, because the supporting documents submitted by the IMF included transcripts of public statements (ibid., items 773, 780–2) made by STPS minister Javier Lozano Alarcón in 2007–10 in which he referred specifically to the problem of protection contracts and puppet unions in Mexico — materials that cast substantial doubt on the blanket denials made by the STPS in responding to the IMF complaint — the ILO panel did insist that the Mexican government clarify its position in this regard.

Assessing the Impact of Transnational Alliances

International actions in support of Mexican workers' rights have taken on new prominence since the 1990s. For some Mexican labour organizations, transnational alliances with unions and labour-rights groups in the United States and Canada have become an important additional power resource in their struggles to defend union members' interests and challenge unfavourable government policies. Although some of these coalitions emphasized more traditional union-to-union solidarity actions focused on workplace issues in a particular company or industrial sector, the most significant of these cross-border alliances have mobilized around grievance petitions filed with the NAALC institutions or the ILO. The availability of these institutional spaces has often been an important catalyst for transnational action.

noted that, in the interest of promoting transparency and workers' knowledge about their employment conditions and union representation, the Federal Conciliation and Arbitration Board (JFCA) began a programme in 2003 to digitalize collective contracts, sectoral worker-employer agreements and internal labour regulations and to make them publicly available on the Internet (ILO, 2011, items 829–30).

Even though none of the 39 NAALC proceedings initiated between 1994 and 2010 ever advanced from ministerial consultations to the penalty phase, they proved a highly effective way of focusing international attention on labour-rights problems in Mexico — a necessary but insufficient condition for effecting change in public policy. There is, moreover, evidence that some of these cases have helped bring about (albeit with some delay) change in such areas as the Mexican government's positions on pre-employment pregnancy testing and the use of secret ballots in union representation elections.[46] The Han Young case on freedom of association did result in the recognition of an independent union, but gains of this kind proved particularly difficult to defend over time — and multiple submissions to the US NAO on freedom-of-association issues did little to disturb those elements of the broader Mexican state-labour relations regime that preserve the established workplace position of government-allied unions. More generally, ensuring that any policy changes brought about through NAALC proceedings actually remain in effect is a major challenge in a country in which the rule of law is weak and corruption and lobbying by employers' groups and old-style labour organizations often impede meaningful reform.

It is important to note in this context that the incidence of NAALC submissions declined significantly after 2000. Whereas there were 24 NAO filings between 1994 and 2000, only 14 cases were initiated between 2001 and 2008.[47] Many Canadian, Mexican and US unions and labour-rights groups expressed growing frustration with a costly grievance process that offered few immediate protections for the workers and unions directly involved. Moreover, they concluded that, with pro-business presidential administrations in office in both the United States (George W. Bush, 2001–09) and in Mexico (Vicente Fox Quesada, 2000–06, and Felipe Calderón Hinojosa, 2006–12), NAO proceedings were even less likely to yield positive results. Submissions to the NAOs still figure among the options available to labour-rights activists seeking to focus public attention on a particular case or issue. Indeed, several of the most high-profile labour conflicts in Mexico — the struggle over proposed reforms to the Federal Labour Law during the Fox administration, the 2006 Pasta de Conchos mine disaster and the assault on the Mexican Electricians' Union (SME) in 2009–10 — included NAALC submissions (designated,

---

46 Following the agreement that Mexican and US labour officials reached on the Han Young and ITAPSA/Echlin cases in May 2002, the Federal Conciliation and Arbitration Board began consistently to employ secret ballots in union representation elections. State-level conciliation and arbitration boards also used them more frequently after 2002, but they still did not do so systematically (Alexander, 2005; Nolan García, 2010, p. 16).

47 The decline was sharpest in submissions to the US NAO; there were 16 filings between 1994 and 2000, but only seven between 2001 and 2008. Submissions to the Canadian and Mexican NAOs were divided roughly equally between the 1994–2000 and 2001–08 periods. Authors' calculations based on information in U.S. Department of Labor, 2010.

respectively, US NAO 2005-01, 2006-01 and 2010-01).[48] But there is little doubt that this avenue of recourse has declined in utility over time.

Petitions that transnational alliances have filed with the ILO since the mid-1990s have also generated substantial international awareness of labour-rights issues in Mexico. Public attention and international condemnation do not necessarily produce policy change — despite assurances by the Mexican government that it has never failed to follow the recommendations of the ILO's Committee on Freedom of Association (ILO, 2011, items 846, 886). Nevertheless, there is evidence that transnational campaigns linked to ILO proceedings have sometimes had an impact on Mexican government policy and even on the actions of private firms. For example, in 1995 the Committee on Freedom of Association found in favour of Mexican complainants who had argued that provisions of the Federal Law for Public Service Workers (LFTSE) violated ILO convention 87 on freedom of association (which was approved by the Mexican Senate and became part of domestic legislation in 1950) by allowing only one union in each federal government workplace and by requiring that all federal government employees join the Federation of Public Service Workers' Unions (FSTSE) (ILO, 1995, items 243–4). A Mexican labour court accepted the ILO's recommendation in 1996, and in 1999 the Supreme Court voted unanimously to repeal these provisions of the LFTSE (La Botz, 1999).

Similarly, as one of its contributions to the 'International Campaign Against Protection Contracts', the Canadian labour-rights group Maquila Solidarity Network put forward a series of proposals on steps that major apparel companies should take to ensure greater respect for freedom of association in their Mexican supplier factories. As a result, a number of international garment firms active in the Mexico Committee of the Multi-Fibre Arrangement Forum agreed to implement at least some of these proposals, including requiring suppliers to give workers access to their collective bargaining agreements.[49]

However uncertain the achievements of transnational labour alliances might sometimes appear, the most important development of all since the early 1990s has been the consolidation of this new form of social capital. One should certainly not underestimate the obstacles to effective transnational labour action (Carr, 1996, pp. 218–25). Nevertheless, cross-border networks among some labour organizations have proved quite durable, such as the links forged among the UE, the FAT and the CUSWA (Kay, 2011, pp. 171–83). These ties have been especially important in both material and political terms for independent Mexican labour organizations like the FAT, which

---

48 The SME and its international union and human-rights organization allies filed supplemental submissions with the Canadian and US NAOs in, respectively, October and November 2011 (www.solidaritycenter.org/content.asp?contentid=1324).

49 Authors' email communication on 5 October 2011 with Lynda Yanz, director of the Maquila Solidarity Network, Toronto, Canada.

featured prominently in many of the transnational unionization campaigns in the *maquiladora* industry from the mid-1990s onward.[50] But even when transnational relationships do not become fully institutionalized, contacts and alliances forged at an earlier time may be revived as new challenges appear (as in the case of the SNTMMSRM and SME conflicts).[51] What is most important is that the memory and practice of cross-border collaboration remain strong, even if the concrete results achieved in any particular case are modest.

---

50 Despite such support, however, in 2010 the FAT only represented approximately 35,000 workers (National Union of Workers [UNT] membership roster dated 21 Aug. 2010).

51 On the basis of their solidarity collaboration, in June 2010 the USWA and the SNTMMSRM announced the formation of a cross-border commission to explore the possibility of creating a single union (www.workersuniting.org/pdf/LOS%20MINEROS-USW_Joint%20 Declaration_06-20-10_FINAL-Sigs.pdf).

Chapter Six
Conclusion

Since the 1980s the Mexican organized labour movement has declined substantially in size, organizational coherence, bargaining strength and political influence. Economic restructuring in both the private and public sectors reduced union densities and placed organized workers on the defensive in negotiations with employers over wages, benefits and working conditions. Historic shifts in government policy toward labour and a general increase in employer resistance to union influence in the workplace (and to unionization more generally) also exacted a heavy toll. The effect on workers' economic and social welfare was highly consequential because unions continue to have a positive impact on wage and fringe benefit levels and on working conditions. Indeed, despite significant gains in labour productivity in the manufacturing industry, the past three decades have witnessed a sharp decline in the inflation-adjusted value of minimum wages, prolonged stagnation in worker incomes, reduced employment opportunities in the formal sector of the economy, and declining union influence over industrial relations policies. The proliferation of 'ghost unions' and 'employer protection contracts' has blocked grassroots organizing and severely constrained efforts by rank-and-file union members to defend their interests in the workplace.

Although economic restructuring and more consistently pro-business government policies radically altered the environment in which all trade unions operate, the impact on specific labour organizations has varied considerably. Those that were hardest hit were government-allied unions like those historically grouped in the Labour Congress (CT), for which the withdrawal of reliable government support and the consequent loss of privileged access to public resources were serious blows. Many (although not all) of these unions experienced substantial membership losses, and their leaders suffered a severe loss of credibility with rank-and-file union members. That wrenching economic and political change did not have an even more debilitating effect on organizations like the Confederation of Mexican Workers (CTM) was due largely to a legal regime and the persistence of well-institutionalized state-labour practices whose origins can be traced to the years immediately following the Mexican Revolution of 1910–20. Indeed, the fact that the CTM remains Mexico's largest labour confederation — and that it therefore retains value as a political ally — is principally due to the advantages it still draws from the representational monopolies its affiliates hold in the workplace and from its continued dominance over labour positions on such tripartite bodies as federal- and state-level conciliation and arbitration boards.

In contrast, some unions have navigated successfully Mexico's momentous economic and political transformations and even increased their influence. Among the most conspicuous examples are the Mexican Mining and Metalworkers' Union (SNTMMSRM), the Mexican Petroleum Workers' Union (Sindicato de Trabajadores Petroleros de la República Mexicana, STPRM), the National Education Workers' Union (SNTE) and the Mexican Telephone Workers' Union (STRM), all of which monopolize representation in their respective industries and have preserved or expanded the bargaining leverage they derive from a nationwide organizational structure and control over economically or politically strategic sectors. The prolonged assault by the administrations of President Vicente Fox Quesada (2000–06) and President Felipe Calderón Hinojosa (2006–12) on the leadership of the SNTMMSRM, and especially the Calderón government's devastating attack on the Mexican Electricians' Union (SME), certainly demonstrated that market-based bargaining leverage and even a proven capacity for effective mobilization are insufficient protections against committed government opponents. Nevertheless, one of the principal contradictions of Mexico's democratization process has been that the weakening of the Institutional Revolutionary Party (PRI) and the reduced influence of the heretofore all-powerful federal executive have permitted the leaders of such old-guard unions as the STPRM and the SNTE to maximize the advantages they derive from their unions' large size, financial resources and representational monopolies, thus permitting them to pursue their own goals and operate as veritable barons or baronesses of union fiefdoms.

The fragmentation of the Mexican labour movement has had decidedly mixed political consequences. On the one hand, the declining membership and influence of the Labour Congress have meant that organized labour no longer speaks with a single voice in national policy debates. For example, whereas in the early 1990s the CT and the CTM still spoke for the labour movement as a whole in their defence of public pension programmes and their opposition to individual, privately-managed retirement accounts, in the early 2000s these organizations were effectively absent from negotiations over social-welfare policy changes affecting large portions of the labour movement. Even at its peak influence, the CT was not necessarily a reliable defender of working-class interests in general. Nevertheless, it is significant that industry- or sector-specific unions have become the principal labour voice in debates over issues of broad importance, such as the restructuring of the Social Security Institute for State Workers (ISSSTE) in 2007 or educational policy reform. This shift increases the likelihood that narrow, sectoral concerns (or, even worse, the preferences of individual union leaders) will prevail over more general interests. The opportunity to strike deals with corrupt or unaccountable union leaders also encourages government officials to make policy via closed, intra-elite bargaining rather than through public debate in an open, politically plural legislative session.[1]

Yet the decline of the Labour Congress and the rise of the National Union of Workers (UNT) have also introduced a vital degree of political pluralism in the labour movement that had been absent for several decades. Union members have in addition gained much greater freedom to express their individual partisan preferences in elections. However, these developments have not produced any significant increase in labour's overall policy influence. Nor does increased pluralism in the labour movement fully compensate for the democratic deficit resulting from the fact that most unions remain dominated by entrenched leaders and rank-and-file members have very limited means of holding them accountable for their actions (or inactions).

Moreover, with the significant exception of the SNTE's formation of its own political party, there has been only modest change in labour organizations' partisan alliances. Despite its loss of the presidency in 2000, the PRI has remained the dominant political force in labour matters. This state of affairs reflects both the resilience of long-established PRI-union ties and an apparent lack of sustained interest on behalf of either the centre-right National Action Party (PAN) or the centre-left Party of the Democratic Revolution (PRD) in building stronger union bases. Neither party has sought systematically to develop union support, and there are comparatively few union representatives in these parties' congressional delegations or governing councils. This may not be surprising in the case of the PAN, in view of the strength of its historic links to business interests, but it is in the case of the PRD, which was formed by a wide range of leftist political currents and social organizations.

This overall continuity in union-party relations contrasts sharply with the growing prominence of transnational ties in union affairs. The negotiation of the North American Free Trade Agreement compelled Canadian and US

1 For example, in 2007 there were widespread allegations that Valdemar Gutiérrez Fragoso, secretary-general of the National Union of Social Security Workers (SNTSS), agreed to contract changes modifying the pension rights of new Mexican Social Security Institute (IMSS) employees (obliging them to accept individual retirement accounts managed by private financial institutions) as part of a deal in which federal authorities sought the extradition of his son from Spain, where he had been detained on drug-trafficking charges (http://rebelionsindical.obolog.com/sntss-gobierno-violentan-derechos-humanos-111705; Ravelo, 2006).

trade unions to re-evaluate their links to the Mexican labour movement, and their growing interest in transnational solidarity alliances created a valuable new political resource for the Mexican labour movement. Few organizations have derived as much benefit from international linkages as the Authentic Labour Front (FAT), but the unions involved in some of the most visible labour conflicts in Mexico since the 1990s (including the SNTMMSRM and the SME) have been able to marshal significant international support from leading unions and labour-rights groups in Canada and the United States. Even though institutional venues such as those created by the North American Agreement on Labor Cooperation have declined in relevance, transnational alliances remain an important additional power resource in Mexican unions' attempts to defend their interests and challenge unfavourable government policies.

On balance, one should not be surprised that far-reaching economic restructuring in Mexico adversely affected the organized labour movement; similar processes of market-centred economic reform have posed serious challenges to unionized workers in many countries. What is perhaps more remarkable is that the country's transition to electoral democracy did not have a more significant impact on the established pattern of state-labour relations. One might have anticipated that a more fully democratic political environment, with generally lower levels of repression and reduced presidential powers, would have offered workers expanded opportunities to pressure for the removal of undue legal restrictions on union formation and strikes, as well as to hold government officials more fully accountable for their administration of labour law.

Electoral democratization has expanded individual union members' political choices at the polls, and the National Education Workers' Union has proved especially adept at deploying its large membership and organizational resources to its political advantage. Yet the transition that brought the National Action Party to national power in 2000 did not lead to major changes in state-labour relations.[2] Although the PAN and the PRI viewed the prospect of federal labour law reform from quite different partisan angles, both parties had substantial stakes in preserving state administrative restrictions on worker participation. The Party of the Democratic Revolution's union allies stood to gain the most from loosening state controls. However, the party did not make far-reaching labour relations reform an especially high priority, in part because the party's union allies did not agree on the merits of labour law reform and perhaps because the reduced size of the unionized population offered little prospect

---

2   This outcome revealed the limitations of those analyses that emphasize the incorporation of organized labour in the PRI as the basis for political control over labour in Mexico. See, for example, Collier and Collier, 1991, pp. 202, 416–9.

of electoral gain by cultivating this particular constituency.[3] Of course, one crucial obstacle in this regard was the hard political fact that many old-style unions maintained their allegiance to the PRI, whose own political resilience held open the prospect of a future return to the presidency and perhaps a full restoration of the alliance on which these unions had so long depended.[4]

Although multiparty electoral competition has had a surprisingly modest impact on state-labour dynamics, other aspects of regime democratization have had important consequences for labour politics. The growing autonomy and assertiveness of the judiciary are especially significant in this regard. In several of the specific conflicts examined in this book (including those involving the Mexican Mining and Metalworkers' Union and the Han Young union), judicial authorities sought — albeit with limited success — to constrain the administrative discretion of government labour officials. More generally, Supreme Court rulings on such matters as freedom of association for public-sector workers, the constitutionality of separation exclusion clauses in collective contracts, and secret balloting in union representation elections have had palpable political effects.[5] For example, the court's 1999 ruling on public-sector unionization prompted major secessions from the theretofore-powerful Federation of Public Sector Workers' Unions (FSTSE) and led to the creation of the Democratic Federation of Public Service Workers' Unions (FDSSP). This same decision also underpinned the formation in 2011 of the Independent Union of Mexican Education Workers (Sindicato Independiente de Trabajadores de la Educación de México) as a rival to the SNTE. Judicial actions such as these have not yet guaranteed a dependable rule of law in labour affairs, but the judiciary does now operate as a partial counterweight to abuses of executive branch authority.[6]

3   The SME, for example, opposed labour code reform in the 1990s (Bensusán, 2000, p. 430).
     The experience of partisan change at the state level also suggests that, once in power, former opposition parties find it advantageous to employ their control (via the appointment of government representatives) over conciliation and arbitration boards to their own partisan advantage, a calculation that constitutes a further obstacle to state-labour relations reform. For an assessment of the PRD's record in this area in the Federal District, see Alcalde Justiniani, Bensusán and Pineda, 2008, pp. 9–13.
     An opinion poll conducted among federal deputies in 2007 found that they ranked labour law reform lower as a priority than any other major pending reform, including constitutional, tax, energy, pension and electoral reforms (*Reforma*, 14 May 2007, p. 6).

4   Throughout the 2000–12 period, the PRI continued to hold the largest single block of seats in the federal Congress, and it consistently controlled the largest number of state governorships at a time when governors played an increasingly prominent role in national political affairs.

5   The court's 2008 ruling on union representation elections specified that 'workers must cast a personal, free, direct and secret vote' and established detailed criteria regarding how conciliation and arbitration boards must organize such proceedings (ILO, 2011, item 820).

6   In June 2011 the Supreme Court sought to restrict federal labour officials' discretionary authority in the recognition of union election results by ruling that the Ministry of Labour and Social Welfare (STPS) must limit its review to evidence concerning whether elections

These developments are highly consequential because the removal of overly restrictive legal and administrative controls on union formation and union activities is an essential first step in the democratization of state-labour relations. Eliminating contract-based separation exclusion clauses and providing employees with easy access to information concerning union registration and collective contracts also contribute to union democratization by potentially enhancing the power of rank-and-file members. The declining prospect that the Congress will enact progressive labour law reform makes the Supreme Court's actions in these areas all the more important.

Yet the broader goals of democratizing governance in labour organizations and in the workplace face both practical barriers and the constraints rooted in the segmented quality of pluralist democracy itself (Middlebrook, 2009, p. 419). In a political democracy, the effective guarantee of citizens' individual political rights — including freedoms of expression and association, and especially protection against arbitrary state action — necessarily means that the state's capacity to transform authority relations in various non-governmental spheres is constrained. State-led efforts to bring about such changes are in practice often viewed as illegitimate transgressions of the limits that societal actors impose on governmental authority. As a consequence, a central paradox of pluralist democracy is that decidedly illiberal authority patterns may prevail in the workplace, in labour organizations or in other such non-governmental arenas even while democratic norms govern exchanges in the public sphere.

There is, however, a far more immediate obstacle to the democratization of the Mexican labour movement and of state-labour relations more generally. Underlying the PAN administrations' labour policies (and those of their PRI predecessors since the 1980s) was the fundamental reality that the economic model in place in Mexico since the 1980s relies heavily on low wages, compliant unions, few strikes and strong employer control over workplace industrial relations. The export of low-value-added manufactured goods to the United States from *maquiladora*-style production facilities has remained the centrepiece of national economic strategy, even though China's entry into the World Trade Organization in 2001 and its progressive encroachment on Mexico's main export market led to declining employment in the *maquiladora* sector and starkly revealed the limits of this approach. Other Latin American countries based their international comparative advantage on the export of high-value-added goods and/or primary products, with the goal of expanding their domestic markets and eventually reducing their potential vulnerability to export disruptions. In contrast, Mexican policymakers have persisted on an economic path that has left little scope for innovation in industrial relations.

have been held in accordance with a union's statutes. (A minority of the justices participating in the 6–5 ruling argued that the STPS had no authority at all to intervene in internal union matters.) The STPS, however, interpreted the decision as a validation of its established practices (Aranda, 2011b; Muñoz Rios, 2011).

Mexico's experience since the 1980s has thus confirmed the essential compatibility between market-centred economic policies and state-labour practices rooted in the country's authoritarian past. The economic and social costs of this perverse combination have been extremely high — manifested in the very slow growth of formal-sector employment and the relative expansion of the informal sector, the proliferation of 'ghost unions' and 'employer protection contracts' that impede grassroots organizing and efforts to strengthen workers' bargaining power vis-à-vis employers, and growing wage and social inequalities. What remains unclear is whether this economic model's evident failure to produce well-paid, skilled jobs in sufficient numbers to satisfy the country's development needs will in time lead to a serious reconsideration not only of established macroeconomic and industrial relations policies, but also of the value of interlocutors in the labour arena with different power resources and the capacity to propel the economy along a higher-value, internationally competitive path. The severe discredit of labour institutions, and the loss of legitimacy and effectiveness that most Mexican trade unions have suffered as instruments for reducing inequality, underscore the urgency of defining an alternative political economy.[7]

Transforming the inherited state-labour relations regime remains, then, a central item on Mexico's uncompleted democracy agenda. The impetus for change must come from those political parties and non-governmental organizations committed to deepening democracy, existing representative labour organizations with a strong membership base, and employers who recognize that improved socio-economic equity is a prerequisite for sustainable economic growth. Reformers face two main challenges. First, they must forge a new social pact centred on expansion of the domestic market, improved socio-economic equity and more democratic workplace relations. Establishing an explicit link between gains in labour productivity and higher remuneration must be a key element of this pact. So long as Mexico seeks to compete in the global economy by artificially suppressing wage levels, there will be little incentive for employers to enhance worker skills or innovate technologically (Palma, 2011, appendix 2). To the extent that raising productivity requires changes in labour law that facilitate flexible contracting and working practices, modifications of this kind must be balanced by legal reforms that encourage the emergence of more representative trade unions capable of defending

---

7 A poll commissioned by *Reforma* newspaper in April 2007 found that only 32 per cent of survey respondents held a favourable ('good' or 'very good') opinion of trade unions, whereas 39 per cent of respondents held an unfavourable ('bad' or 'very bad') opinion of them. Trade union leaders were held in even greater disrepute; 52 per cent of respondents viewed them negatively, compared to only 20 per cent of respondents who held a favourable opinion of them. A plurality (44 per cent) of the union members included in the survey felt that unions harmed workers, whereas only 36 per cent felt that unions benefited workers (*Reforma*, 1 May 2007, p. 6).

employees' legitimate interests in the workplace and promoting new forms of social protection (for example, unemployment insurance to protect workers against the risks posed by heightened instability in the job market). It is essential that both employers and government policymakers recognize the constructive role that membership-accountable unions can play in formulating strategies to increase productivity and equitably distribute the resulting economic gains.[8]

The second challenge is to build democratic rule of law in the labour sector. The collective rights that workers won in the Mexican Revolution have long been obstructed by government officials, manipulated by employers or captured by unaccountable union leaders seeking to sustain their position on the basis of artificial majorities. Labour rights are human rights; their realization is integral to the construction of a democratic society based on the rule of law.[9] Workers must in practice enjoy the full and autonomous right to organize themselves, freely elect their representatives and hold them to account for their actions, negotiate with employers — and, when circumstances require, exercise the right to strike in defence of their interests. Both workers and employers would benefit from the certainties that would derive from an impartial, efficient labour justice system and competent workplace inspections. It is long past time to recast the institutional arrangements inherited from Mexico's post-revolutionary authoritarian regime and restore legitimate rights to workers, guaranteeing — without regard to particular organizational or partisan affiliation — the universal rights associated with the idea of citizenship.

8   For empirical evidence on this point from Mexico and other countries, see Freeman and Medoff, 1984; Aidt and Tzannatos, 2002; Fairris and Levine, 2004; Fairris, 2006; Hayter and Weinberg, 2011.

9   One significant development in this regard was the elimination in June 2011 of the constitutional provision (article 102[B], paragraph 3) that barred the National Human Rights Commission (CNDH) from addressing labour issues. See 'Decreto por el que se modifica la denominación del Capítulo I del Título Primero y reforma varios artículos de la Constitución Política de los Estados Unidos Mexicanos', *Diario Oficial de la Federación*, 10 June 2011 (http://dof.gob.mx).

Bibliography

Aguayo Quezada, Sergio (2010) 'Sin contrapesos', *Reforma*, 2 June, p. 13.

Aguayo Quezada, Sergio, and Alberto Serdán (2009) 'Es Gordillo maestra del presupuesto', *Reforma*, 13 Dec., p. 6.

Aguilar García, Javier (2001) *La población trabajadora y sindicalizada en México en el período de la globalización* (Mexico City: Instituto de Investigaciones Sociales, Universidad Nacional Autónoma de México/ Fondo de Cultura Económica).

Aidt, Toke, and Zafiris Tzannatos (2002) *Unions and Collective Bargaining: Economic Effects in a Global Environment* (Washington, DC: World Bank).

Alcalde Justiniani, Arturo (2009) 'Acometida contra el SME', *La Jornada*, 8 Oct., p. 17.

— (2011a) 'Iniciativa priísta: una traición a los trabajadores', *La Jornada*, 12 Mar., p. 22.

— (2011b) 'La reforma laboral y la OIT', *La Jornada*, 26 Mar., p. 17.

— (2011c) 'Cinco conclusiones sobre propuestas laborales PRI-PAN', *La Jornada*, 9 Apr., p. 17.

Alcalde Justiniani, Arturo, et al. (2003) *Reforma laboral: una iniciativa para favorecer al corporativismo* (Mexico City: Instituto de Investigaciones Económicas, Universidad Nacional Autónoma de México).

Alcalde Justiniani, Arturo, Graciela Bensusán and Patricia Juan Pineda (2008) *Derechos colectivos y opacidad informativa*, Cuadernos de Investigación No. 3 (Mexico City: Centro de Investigación Laboral y Asesoría Sindical).

Alexander, Robin (2005) 'FAT Obtains First Secret Ballot Election; International Observers Report on Experience', *Mexican Labor News and Analysis*, vol. 10, no. 6 (June) (www.ueinternational.org/MLNA).

Álvarez Béjar, Alejandro (1991) 'Economic Crisis and the Labor Movement in Mexico', in Kevin J. Middlebrook (ed.), *Unions, Workers, and the State in Mexico* (La Jolla, CA: Center for U.S.-Mexican Studies, University of California, San Diego), pp. 27–55.

Aranda, Jesús (2011a) 'Rechaza SCJN conocer amparos de electricistas contra extinción de LFC', *La Jornada en línea*, 4 May.

— (2011b) 'Limita Corte a STPS en toma de nota a órganos sindicales', *La Jornada en línea*, 20 June.

Avilés, Karina (2011a) 'En 2006 apoyé a Felipe Calderón y pactamos reformas, afirma Gordillo', *La Jornada*, 30 June, pp. 2–4.

— (2011b) 'Crean nuevo sindicato magisterial', *La Jornada en línea*, 7 Feb.

— (2011c) 'Insiste Gordillo en que se aplique una auditoría al Issste', *La Jornada*, 30 June, p. 3.

Aziz, Alberto (2007) 'Reforma al ISSSTE', *El Universal*, 20 Mar. (Sección Editorial).

Bacon, David (1998) 'Maquiladoras Strike Continues on US-Mexican Border', Inter Press Service, 4 June.

— (2000) 'Strikers Beaten at NAFTA-sponsored Meeting' (http://dbacon. igc.org/Mexico/17StrikersBeaten.htm).

Banco de México (2009) 'Principales indicadores salariales en México' (www. banxico.org.mx).

Bandy, Joe (2005) 'So What Is to Be Done? Maquila Justice Movements, Transnational Justice, and Dynamics of Resistance', in Kathryn Kopinak (ed.), *The Social Costs of Industrial Growth in Northern Mexico* (La Jolla, CA: Center for U.S.-Mexican Studies, University of California, San Diego), pp. 309–42.

Beaulieu, Eugene, Liliana Meza González and Raymond Robertson (2010) 'Trade and Labor Markets in the Three NAFTA Countries', in Ismael Aguilar et al. (eds.), *Senderos de la integración silenciosa en América del Norte* (Mexico City: El Colegio de México/Centro de Investigaciones sobre América del Norte, Universidad Nacional Autónoma de México), pp. 41–68.

Bensusán, Graciela (1992) 'Institucionalización laboral en México: los años de la definición jurídica, 1917–1931.' PhD thesis, Facultad de Ciencias Políticas y Sociales, Universidad Nacional Autónoma de México.

— (2000) *El modelo mexicano de regulación laboral* (Mexico City: Plaza y Valdés).

— (2003) 'Alternancia política y continuidad laboral: las limitaciones de la propuesta del CCE/CT', in Arturo Alcalde Justiniani et al. (eds.), *Reforma laboral: una iniciativa para favorecer al corporativismo* (Mexico City: Instituto de Investigaciones Económicas, Universidad Nacional Autónoma de México).

— (2004) 'A New Scenario for Mexican Trade Unions: Changes in the Structure of Political and Economic Opportunities', in Kevin J. Middlebrook (ed.), *Dilemmas of Political Change in Mexico* (London: Institute of Latin American Studies, University of London/Center for U.S.-Mexican Studies, University of California, San Diego), pp. 237–85.

— (2005a) 'Renovación sindical y democracia: los límites de la alternancia', in Alberto Aziz Nassif and Jorge Alonso Sánchez (eds.), *El estado mexicano: herencias y cambios*, vol. III, *Sociedad civil y diversidad* (Mexico City: Centro de Investigaciones y Estudios Superiores en Antropología Social/Editorial Miguel Ángel Porrúa), pp. 97–139.

— (2005b) 'El Sindicato Mexicano de Electricistas y la reestructuración laboral en Luz y Fuerza del Centro', *Revista Mexicana de Sociología*, vol. 67, no. 1, pp. 543–91.

— (2007a) 'Los determinantes institucionales de los contratos de protección', in Alfonso Bouzas Ortiz and Luis Oliver Reyes Ramos (eds.), *Contratación colectiva de protección en México: informe a la Organización Regional Interamericana de Trabajadores* (Mexico City: Universidad Nacional Autónoma de México/Confederación Internacional de Organizaciones Sindicales Libres-Organización Regional Interamericana de Trabajadores), pp. 13–48.

— (2007b) 'Normas, hechos y percepciones: la situación laboral en la industria del vestido en México' (Mexico City: Fundación Levi-Strauss/ Universidad Autónoma Metropolitana-Xochimilco).

— (2008) 'Regulaciones laborales, calidad de los empleos y modelos de inspección: México en el contexto latinoamericano', Research paper LC/ MEX/L.861 (Mexico City: Comisión Económica para América Latina y el Caribe).

— (2009) 'Estándares laborales y calidad de los empleos en América Latina', *Revista Perfiles Latinoamericanos*, vol. 34 (July–Dec.), pp. 13–49.

— (2010a) 'El alcance y la viabilidad de la reforma laboral', *El Universal*, 12 Feb. 2010, p. 22.

— (2010b) 'El desacuerdo de fondo en la reforma laboral', *El Universal*, 30 Mar., p. 20.

— (2011a) 'Necesidad y viabilidad de la postergada reforma de la legislación laboral.' Unpublished manuscript.

— (2011b) 'La reforma laboral priísta', *El Universal*, 18 Mar.

Bensusán, Graciela, and Kevin J. Middlebrook (2012) 'Organized Labor and Politics in Mexico', in Roderic Ai Camp (ed.), *Oxford Handbook of Mexican Politics* (New York: Oxford University Press), pp. 335–64.

Bensusán, Graciela, and Luis Arturo Tapia (2011) 'El SNTE: una experiencia singular en el sindicalismo mexicano', *El Cotidiano*, no. 168 (July–Aug.), pp. 17–32.

Bensusán, Graciela, and Maria Lorena Cook (2003) 'Political Transition and Labor Revitalization in Mexico', in Daniel B. Cornfield and Holly J. McCammon (eds.), *Labor Revitalization: Global Perspectives and New Initiatives* (Oxford: Elsevier JAI), pp. 229–67.

Bertranou, Julián F. (1995) 'La política de la reforma a la seguridad social en México: análisis de la formulación del Sistema de Ahorro para el Retiro', *Estudios Sociológicos*, vol. 13, no. 37, pp. 3–23.

Bizberg, Ilán (2003) 'El sindicalismo en el fin de régimen', *Foro Internacional*, no. 171 (Jan.–Mar.), pp. 215–48.

Blanke, Svenja, Inés González and Leticia Hernández (2008) *Informe: campaña internacional contra los contratos de protección patronal en México* (Mexico City: Fundación Friedrich Ebert Stiftung).

Blum, Roberto E. (1997) 'Mexico's New Politics: The Weight of the Past', *Journal of Democracy*, vol. 4, no. 8, pp. 28–42.

'Boletín de la Presidencia' (2009) *México Actúa*, no. 140, 13 Oct.

Boltvinik, Julio (2003) 'Welfare, Inequality, and Poverty in Mexico, 1970–2000', in Kevin J. Middlebrook and Eduardo Zepeda (eds.), *Confronting Development: Assessing Mexico's Economic and Social Policy Challenges* (Stanford, CA: Stanford University Press/Center for U.S.-Mexican Studies, University of California, San Diego), pp. 385–446.

Bouzas Ortiz, José Alfonso, and Germán Reyes Gaytán (2010) *Análisis sucinto de los tópicos más importantes de las propuestas de reforma laboral 2010: PAN y PRD*. Cuaderno de Análisis Político (Mexico City: Fundación Friedrich Ebert Stiftung).

Bouzas Ortiz, José Alfonso, and Luis Oliver Reyes Ramos (eds.) (2007) *Contratación colectiva de protección en México: informe a la Organización Regional Interamericana de Trabajadores* (Mexico City: Universidad Nacional Autónoma de México/Confederación Internacional de Organizaciones Sindicales Libres-Organización Regional Interamericana de Trabajadores).

Brito, Luis (2010) 'Va el sindicato por reinstalación', *Reforma*, 6 July, p. 2.

Burgess, Katrina (2004) *Parties and Unions in the New Global Economy* (Pittsburgh, PA: University of Pittsburgh Press).

Cameron, Maxwell A., and Brian W. Tomlin (2000) *The Making of NAFTA: How the Deal Was Done* (Ithaca, NY: Cornell University Press).

Camp, Roderic Ai (2011) *Mexican Political Biographies, 1935–2009*, 4th ed. (Austin: University of Texas Press).

Cano, Arturo, and Alberto Aguirre (2007) *Doña Perpetua: el poder y la opulencia de Elba Esther Gordillo* (Mexico City: Grijalbo).

Cantú, Jesús (2011) 'Maromas, invectivas y clientelismo electoral', *Proceso* (online edition), 18 July.

Carr, Barry (1996) 'Crossing Borders: Labor Internationalism in the Era of NAFTA', in Gerardo Otero (ed.), *Neoliberalism Revisited: Economic Restructuring and Mexico's Political Future* (Boulder, CO.: Westview Press).

Caulfield, Norman (1998) *Mexican Workers and the State: From the Porfiriato to NAFTA* (Forth Worth, TX: Texas Christian University Press).

Centro de Acción y Reflexión Laboral (2007) 'El gobierno del cambio, un fracaso para las y los trabajadores. El nuevo sexenio panista, lo mismo pero más precario', in *X informe sobre violaciones a los derechos humanos laborales durante 2006* (Mexico City: Centro de Acción y Reflexión Laboral), pp. 36–9.

Centro de Estudios de las Finanzas Públicas (2007) 'Aspectos relevantes de la reforma al ISSSTE', *Nota informativa*, 23 Mar.

Centro de Investigación para el Desarrollo, A.C. (2011a) 'Reforma laboral: statu quo y la estrategia electoral', *Semana Política*, no. 372 (27 Apr.).

— (2011b) 'Fuero militar: vida a la Constitución', *Semana Política*, no. 383 (14 July).

Chacón, Rolando (2010) 'Anuncia Lozano plan de reactivación', *Reforma*, 8 June, p. 1.

Chávez Sañudo, Andrés (2004) 'Luz y Fuerza del Centro: un camino hacia la modernización.' Unpublished manuscript.

Ciudad, Adolfo (2002) *Reformas laborales y procesos de integración en los países de la OEA: 1980–2000* (Lima: Oficina Internacional del Trabajo).

Clifton, Judith (2000) *The Politics of Telecommunications in Mexico: Privatization and State-Labour Relations, 1982–95* (New York: St. Martin's Press).

Collier, Ruth Berins, and David Collier (1991) *Shaping the Political Arena: Critical Junctures, the Labor Movement, and Regime Dynamics in Latin America* (Princeton, NJ: Princeton University Press).

Collombat, Thomas (2011) 'Several Souths: The Dynamics of the International Labour Movement in the Americas'. PhD diss., Department of Political Science, Carleton University.

Confederación de Trabajadores de México (1996) *Principios de la nueva cultura laboral* (Mexico City: Confederación de Trabajadores de México).

Confederación Patronal de la República Mexicana (1989) 'Propuestas preliminares de la Confederación Patronal de la República Mexicana presentadas en junio de 1989 para la discusión del anteproyecto de una nueva Ley Federal del Trabajo' (Mexico City: Confederación Patronal de la República Mexicana).

Cuenca, Alberto (2010) 'Investigan pagos a miembros del SNTE', *El Universal*, 31 Mar., p. 4.

Dávila Capalleja, Enrique Rafael (1997) 'Mexico: The Evolution and Reform of the Labor Market', in Sebastian Edwards and Nora Claudia Lustig (eds.), *Labor Markets in Latin America: Combining Social Protection with Market Flexibility* (Washington, DC: Brookings Institution).

Davis, Charles L. (1989) *Working-Class Mobilization and Political Control: Venezuela and Mexico* (Lexington, KY: University Press of Kentucky).

De la Garza Toledo, Enrique (ed.), (1998) *La privatización en México: consecuencias sociales y laborales* (Mexico City: Instituto de Estudios de la Revolución Democrática).

De la Garza Toledo, Enrique (2003) 'La crisis de los modelos sindicales en México y sus opciones', in Enrique de la Garza Toledo and Carlos Salas (eds.), *La situación del trabajo en México, 2003* (Mexico City: Plaza y Valdés), pp. 349–77.

— (2006a) 'Apéndice: la polémica acerca de la tasa de sindicalización en México', in Enrique de la Garza Toledo and Carlos Salas (eds.), *La situación del trabajo en México, 2006* (Mexico City: Plaza y Valdés), pp. 486–96.

— (2006b) 'Los proyectos de reforma laboral de la UNT y del CT-CCE', in Enrique de la Garza Toledo and Carlos Salas (eds.), *La situación del trabajo en México, 2006* (Mexico City: Plaza y Valdés), pp. 497–546.

— (2012) 'La polémica sobre la tasa de afiliación sindical revisada', in Enrique de la Garza (ed.), *La situación del trabajo en México durante la crisis actual* (Mexico City: Plaza y Valdés).

Del Valle, Sonia (2010a) 'Rechaza SNTE lista de 10 mil comisionados', *Reforma*, 13 July, p. 5.

— (2010b) 'Ofrecen a SNTE hasta secretarías', *Reforma*, 28 June, p. 6.

Díaz, Ariane (2011) 'Ex secretario particular de Gordillo y su hija, nuevos líderes de Panal', *La Jornada en línea*, 30 June.

Dillon, Sam (1998) 'Bias Said to Hurt Independent Mexican Unions', *New York Times*, 30 Apr. (online edition).

Dion, Michelle L. (2010) *Workers and Welfare: Comparative Institutional Change in Twentieth-Century Mexico* (Pittsburgh, PA: University of Pittsburgh Press).

El Universal (2009) 'Tres miradas de la situación de LyFC', 12 Oct. (www. ElUniversal.com.mx).

Espinosa-Vega, Marco A., and Tapen Sinha (2000) 'A Primer and Assessment of Social Security Reform in Mexico', *Federal Reserve Bank of Atlanta Economic Review*, vol. 85, no. 1, pp. 1–23.

Esquinca, Marco Tulio, and Javier Melgoza Valdivia (2006) 'La afiliación sindical y premio salarial en México', in Enrique de la Garza Toledo and Carlos Salas (eds.), *La situación del trabajo en México, 2006* (Mexico City: Plaza y Valdés), pp. 459–85.

Fairris, David (2006) *What Do Unions Do in Mexico?* (Mexico City: Universidad Iberoamericana).

Fairris, David, and Edward Levine (2004) 'Declining Union Density in Mexico, 1984–2000', *Monthly Labor Review*, no. 127 (Sept.), pp. 3–10.

Fairris, David, Gurleen Popli, and Eduardo Zepeda (2001) 'Minimum Wages and the Wage Structure in Mexico', paper presented at the international congress of the Latin American Studies Association, Washington, DC, Sept.

Finbow, Robert G. (2006) *The Limits of Regionalism: NAFTA's Labour Accord* (Aldershot: Ashgate).

Freeman, Richard B., and James L. Medoff (1984) *What Do Unions Do?* (New York: Basic Books).

Fuentes, Víctor (2010) 'Anuncia Secretaría del Trabajo desconocimiento a Esparza', *Reforma*, 10 June, p. 2.

García, Imelda (2008) 'Pierde la CTM 34% de sus aliados', *El Mañana*, 1 May (www.elmanana.com.mx).

Garduño, Eduardo (2009) 'AN va por reforma que obligue a los sindicatos a rendir cuentas', *La Jornada*, 29 Dec., p. 3.

Gatica Lara, Ignacio (2007) 'El corporativismo sindical mexicano en su encrucijada', *El Cotidiano*, no. 143 (May–June), pp. 71–9.

Gómez, Leslie (2010a) 'Agoniza CTM', *Reforma*, 23 Feb., p. 1.

— (2010b) 'Exige SME a CFE reconoce contrato', *Reforma*, 14 July, p. 8.

Gómez Tagle, Silvia (1997) *La transición inconclusa: treinta años de elecciones en México* (Mexico City: El Colegio de México).

González, Susana (2010) 'Más de 901 mil empleos perdidos en el primer trimestre: Inegi', *La Jornada*, 23 May, p. 23.

Hathaway, Dale (2000) *Allies Across the Border: Mexico's "Authentic Labor Front" and Global Solidarity* (Cambridge, MA: Southend Press).

Hayter, Susan, and Bradley Weinberg (2011) 'Mind the Gap: Collective Bargaining and Wage Inequality', in Susan Hayter (ed.), *The Role of Collective Bargaining in the Global Economy: Negotiating for Social Justice* (Geneva: International Labour Office), pp. 136–86.

Hernández, César (2007) *La reforma cautiva: inversión, trabajo y empresa en el sector eléctrico mexicano* (Mexico City: Centro de Investigación del Desarrollo, A.C.).

Hernández Laos, Enrique (2006) 'La productividad en México: origen y distribución (1960–2002)', in Enrique de la Garza Toledo and Carlos Salas (eds.), *La situación del trabajo en México, 2006* (Mexico City: Plaza y Valdés), pp. 151–77.

Hernández Navarro, Luis (2011) *Cero en conducta: crónicas de la resistencia magisterial* (Mexico City: Fundación Rosa Luxemburgo y Para Leer en Libertad, A.C.).

Herrera, Fernando, and Javier Melgoza (2003) 'Evolución reciente de la afiliación sindical y la regulación laboral en México', in Enrique de la Garza Toledo and Carlos Salas (eds.), *La situación del trabajo en México, 2003* (Mexico City: Plaza y Valdés), pp. 323–47.

Hughes, Steve, and Nigel Haworth (2010) *The International Labour Organisation: Coming in from the Cold* (London: Routledge).

Human Rights Watch (1996) *No Guarantees: Sex Discrimination in Mexico's Maquiladora Sector, A Human Rights Watch Short Report*, vol. 8, no. 6 (Aug.) (www.hrw.org/reports/1996/Mexi0896.htm).

— (1998) *A Job or Your Rights: Continued Sex Discrimination in Mexico's Maquiladora Sector, A Human Rights Watch Short Report*, vol. 10, no. 1(B) (Dec.) (www.hrw.org/legacy/reports98/women2/).

Instituto Federal Electoral (2006) *Elecciones federales 2006: encuestas y resultados electorales* (Mexico City: Instituto Federal Electoral).

Instituto Nacional de Estadística, Geografía e Informática (INEGI) (2010) *Resultados de la Encuesta Nacional de Ocupación y Empleo (2010)*, Communication 065/10 (INEGI: Aguascalientes, México).

Inter-American Development Bank (1997) *Latin America After a Decade of Reforms* (Washington, DC: Inter-American Development Bank).

International Labour Organization (1995) *Committee on Freedom of Association Report No. 300 (Case No. 1844)*, vol. 78, Series B, no. 3 (Geneva: International Labour Office).

— (2006) *Digest of Decisions and Principles of the Freedom of Association Committee of the Governing Body of the ILO*, fifth (rev.) ed. (Geneva: International Labour Office).

— (2008a) *Global Wage Report, 2008–09: Minimum Wages and Collective Bargaining; Towards Policy Coherence* (Geneva: International Labour Office).

— (2008b) 'Complaints Against the Government of Mexico Presented by the International Metalworkers' Federation (IMF) and the National Union of Miners, Metalworkers, and Allied Workers of the Republic of Mexico (SNTMMSRM)', Report no. 350, Freedom of Association Case no. 2478 (Document vol. XCI, 2008, series B, no. 2).

— (2011) *359th Report of the Committee on Freedom of Association* (Geneva: International Labour Office).

Kay, Tamara (2011) *NAFTA and the Politics of Labor Transnationalism* (New York: Cambridge University Press).

Kohout, Michal (2008) 'The New Labor Culture and Labor Law Reform in Mexico', *Latin American Perspectives*, vol. 35, no. 1, pp. 135–50.

Kurtz, Marcus J. (2004) 'The Dilemmas of Democracy in the Open Economy: Lessons from Latin America', *World Politics*, vol. 56, no. 2, pp. 262–302.

La Botz, Dan (1992) *Mask of Democracy: Labor Suppression in Mexico Today* (Boston: South End Press).

— (1999) 'Mexican Supreme Court Rules that Workers Have Right to Organize Independent Unions in the Public Sector', *Mexican Labor News and Analysis*, vol. 4, no. 10.

— (2000) 'Fox and PRI-controlled Unions Move Toward Accommodation, Alliance', *Mexican Labor News and Analysis*, vol. 5, no. 8.

Langston, Joy (2010) 'El dinosaurio que no murió: el PRI de México', in Elisa Servín (ed.), *Del nacionalismo al neoliberalismo, 1940–1994*. Vol. 6 in Clara García Ayluardo and Ignacio Marván Laborde (eds.), *Historia crítica de las modernizaciones en México* (Mexico City: Fondo de Cultura Económica), pp. 295–344.

Langston, Joy, and Scott Morgenstern (2009) 'Campaigning in an Electoral Authoritarian Regime: The Case of Mexico', *Comparative Politics*, vol. 41, no. 2, pp. 165–81.

Laurell, Asa Cristina (2003) 'The Transformation of Social Policy in Mexico', in Kevin J. Middlebrook and Eduardo Zepeda (eds.), *Confronting Development: Assessing Mexico's Economic and Social Policy Challenges* (Stanford, CA: Stanford University Press/Center for U.S.-Mexican Studies, University of California, San Diego), pp. 320–49.

Lawson, Chappell H., et al. (2000) *Mexican Election Panel Study, 2000* (www.icpsr.umich.edu/icpsrweb/ICPSR/studies/03380).

Lawson, Chappell H., et al. (2006) *The Mexico 2006 Panel Study* (http://web.mit.edu/clawson/www/polisci/research/mexico06/).

Leal, Gustavo (2007) 'ISSSTE: ¿"inexpertos" versus "incrédulos"?' *La Jornada*, 17 Mar., p. 6.

Levenstein, Harvey A. (1971) *Labour Organizations in the United States and Mexico: A History of their Relations* (Westport, CT: Greenwood Press).

Levitsky, Steven, and Scott Mainwaring (2006) 'Organized Labor and Democracy in Latin America', *Comparative Politics*, vol. 39, no. 1, pp. 21–42.

Loaeza, Soledad (2011) 'Elba Ester Gordillo y el juicio de la historia', *Nexos* (online edition), 21 July.

Lustig, Nora (1992) *Mexico: The Remaking of an Economy* (Washington, DC: Brookings Institution).

Luz y Fuerza del Centro (2008) *Acta de la cuarta sesión ordinaria de la Junta de Gobierno del Organismo Decentralizado Luz y Fuerza del Centro*, 5 Dec.

— (2009) 'Evolución de los indicadores del convenio de productividad.' Document.

Luz y Fuerza del Centro/Sindicato Mexicano de Electricistas (2008) *Contrato colectivo de trabajo, 2008–2010.* Document.

Madrid, Raúl (2003) 'Labouring Against Neoliberalism: Unions and Patterns of Reform in Latin America', *Journal of Latin American Studies*, vol. 35, part 1, pp. 53–88.

Malkin, Elisabeth (2009) 'Blackouts Engulf a Capital as Power Play Unfurls', *International Herald Tribune*, 27 Oct., p. 17.

Martínez, Fabiola (2010) 'Condiciona el Gobierno analizar plan del SME a la conclusión del ayuno colectivo', *La Jornada*, 23 July, p. 7.

Martínez, Fabiola, and Patricia Muñoz Rios (2009) 'SME y trabajadores cumplieron el convenio de productividad en promedio en un 92.17%', *La Jornada*, 15 Oct., p. 8.

Martínez, Nurit (2008) 'Buscarán restar poder a Elba', *El Universal*, 26 Mar. (www.eluniversal.com.mx).

Martínez Elorriaga, Ernesto (2011), 'Silvano Aureoles solicita registro como candidato del PRD al gobierno de Michoacán', *La Jornada*, 15 Aug., p. 33.

Mayer, Jean-François (2003) 'The Mexican Federal Labour Law Reform Process, 2001–2003', *Labour, Capital and Society*, vol. 36, no. 1, pp. 72–102.

— (2006) 'Changes in Relations between the State and Independent Unions? Mexico Under the Fox Presidency', *Canadian Journal of Latin American and Caribbean Studies*, vol. 31 (Jan.), pp. 9–35.

McLeod, Dag (2004) *Downsizing the State: Privatization and the Limits of Neoliberal Reform in Mexico* (University Park, PA: Pennsylvania University Press).

Melgoza, Javier, and Rafael Montesinos (2003) 'Representatividad, democracia y legitimidad en el Sindicato Mexicano de Electricistas', in Enrique de la Garza Toledo (ed.), *Reestructuración empresarial, democracia, representatividad y legitimidad sindical en México* (Mexico City: Plaza y Valdés), pp. 139–71.

Méndez, Enrique, and Roberto Garduño (2011a) 'Inicia en comisiones de San Lázaro revisión del dictamen de LFT', *La Jornada en línea*, 17 Mar.

— (2011b) 'La diputación del PRI congela la Ley de Seguridad Nacional', *La Jornada en línea*, 29 Apr.

Middlebrook, Kevin J. (1982) 'International Implications of Labor Change: The Mexican Automobile Industry', in Jorge I. Domínguez (ed.), *Mexico's Political Economy: Challenges at Home and Abroad* (Beverly Hills, CA: Sage Publications), pp. 133–70.

— (1986) 'Political Liberalization in an Authoritarian Regime: The Case of Mexico', in Guillermo O'Donnell, Philippe C. Schmitter and Laurence Whitehead (eds.), *Transitions from Authoritarian Rule: Prospects for Democracy*, Pt. 2, *Latin America* (Baltimore, MD: Johns Hopkins University Press), pp. 123–47.

— (1995) *The Paradox of Revolution: Labor, the State, and Authoritarianism in Mexico* (Baltimore, MD: Johns Hopkins University Press).

— (1997) 'Movimiento obrero y democratización en regímenes posrevolucionarios: las políticas de transición en Nicaragua, Rusia y México', *Foro Internacional*, no. 149, pp. 365–407.

— (2009) 'Caciquismo and Democracy: Mexico and Beyond', *Bulletin of Latin American Research*, vol. 28, no. 3, pp. 411–27.

— (n.d.) 'Worker Rights and the NAFTA Labor Institutions: Free Trade, Social Justice, and North American Integration.' Unpublished manuscript.

Middlebrook, Kevin J., and Eduardo Zepeda (2003) 'On the Political Economy of Mexican Development Policy', in Kevin J. Middlebrook and Eduardo Zepeda (eds.), *Confronting Development: Assessing Mexico's Economic and Social Policy Challenges* (Stanford, CA: Stanford University Press/Center for U.S.-Mexican Studies, University of California, San Diego), pp. 3–52.

— (eds.) (2006) *La industria maquiladora de exportación: ensamble, manufactura y desarrollo económico* (Mexico City: Universidad Autónoma Metropolitana-Azcapotzalco).

Monroy Aguirre, Hilario (2000) 'Obreros con Fox...', *Unomásuno*, 8 Oct.

Moreno-Brid, Juan Carlos, and Jaime Ros (2009) *Development and Growth in the Mexican Economy: A Historical Perspective* (New York: Oxford University Press).

Morris, Stephen D. (1999) 'Corruption and the Mexican Political System: Continuity and Change', *Third World Quarterly*, vol. 20, no. 3, pp. 623–43.

Muñoz Armenta, Aldo (2010) *El sindicalismo mexicano y el voto corporativo: el SNTE y su alianza con el PAN en las elecciones de 2006* (Mexico City: Editorial Universidad Iberoamericana).

Muñoz Rios, Patricia (2007) 'Desbandada masiva de afiliados hace languidecer a las centrales sindicales', *La Jornada*, 4 June, p. 43.

— (2009) 'Se reelige Esparza Flores al frente del SME', *La Jornada en línea*, 3 July.

— (2010a) 'Niega corte amparo al SME, dice STPS', *La Jornada*, 11 June, p. 7.

— (2010b) 'Anuncia Lozano tercera etapa de liquidación de trabajadores del SME', *La Jornada en línea*, 13 July.

— (2011) 'Interpreta Secretaría del Trabajo que validó SCJN verificación que hace de estatutos sindicales', *La Jornada en línea*, 20 June.

Muñoz Rios, Patricia, and Fabiola Martínez (2009) 'Ir contra otros gremios sería autoritarismo, aduce Lozano', *La Jornada*, 15 Oct., p. 7.

— (2011) 'Levanta SME plantón del Zócalo y Esparza recibe la toma de nota', *La Jornada en línea*, 13 Sept.

Muñoz Rios, Patricia, and Leopoldo Ramos (2010) 'Detenidos, dos madres de mineros', *La Jornada*, 8 June, p. 31.

Nolan García, Kimberley A. (2010) *Norms Socialization and NAFTA's Side Accord on Labor*, Documentos de Trabajo No. 206 (Mexico City: Centro de Investigación y Docencia Económicas).

Notimex (2010) 'Por fibra óptica de CFD, Megacable, Telefónica y Televisa ofertan 885 mdp', 27 May.

— (2011) 'CFE, sin capacidad para contratar a miembros del SME: Gobernación', *La Jornada en línea*, 15 Feb.

O'Connor, Anne-Marie (1997) 'Tijuana Union Fight Highlights NAFTA Fears', *Los Angeles Times*, 7 Nov. (online edition).

Pacheco Méndez, Guadalupe, and Juan Reyes del Campillo (1989) 'La estructura sectorial del PRI y las elecciones federales de diputados, 1979–1988', *Revista Sociológica* 11 (Sept.–Dec.), pp. 59–74.

Palma, José Gabriel (2011) 'Homogeneous Middles vs. Heterogeneous Tails and the End of the "Inverted-U": The Share of the Rich is What It's All About', *Cambridge Working Papers in Economics* No. 1111 (www.econ.cam.ac.uk/dae/repec/cam/pdf/cwpe1111.pdf).

Partido Acción Nacional (1995) 'Iniciativa de decreto que reforma a la Ley Federal del Trabajo presentada por el Grupo Parlamentario del Partido Acción Nacional de la LVI Legislatura a la Comisión Permanente del H. Congreso de la Unión.'

— (2002) 'Iniciativa de reforma a la Ley Federal del Trabajo presentada por el Grupo Parlamentario del Partido Acción Nacional de la LVIII Legislatura de la Cámara de Diputados del H. Congreso de la Unión.' 19 Mar.

— (2010) 'Iniciativa de reforma a la Ley Federal del Trabajo presentada por el Grupo Parlamentario del Partido Acción Nacional de la LXI Legislatura de la Cámara de Diputados del H. Congreso de la Unión.' 18 Mar.

Partido de la Revolución Democrática (1998) 'Anteproyecto de reforma a la Constitución Política de los Estados Unidos Mexicanos y la Ley Federal del Trabajo presentado por el Grupo Parlamentario del Partido de la Revolución Democrática de la LVII Legislatura de la Cámara de Diputados del H. Congreso de la Unión.' May.

Partido de la Revolución Democrática/Unión Nacional de Trabajadores (2010) 'Iniciativa de decreto por el que se reforman, derogan y adicionan diversas disposiciones de los artículos 74, 78, 102, 115, 116 y 123 de la Constitución Política de los Estados Unidos Mexicanos a la Ley Federal del Trabajo presentada por el Grupo Parlamentario del Partido de la

Revolución Democrática de la LXI Legislatura de la Cámara de Diputados del H. Congreso de la Unión.' 15 Apr.

Partido Revolucionario Institucional (2010) 'Iniciativa con proyecto de decreto que reforma, deroga y adiciona diversas disposiciones de la Ley Federal del Trabajo a cargo del Grupo Parlamentario del PRI.' Dec.

— (2011) 'Iniciativa que reforma, adiciona y deroga diversas disposiciones de la Ley Federal del Trabajo, a cargo de Tereso Medina Ramírez, Francisco Rojas Gutiérrez, José Ramón Martel López, Isaías González Cuevas y otros 234 diputados del Grupo Parlamentario del PRI.' Mar.

Pastrana, Daniela (2004) 'La CTM: más viva que nunca', *La Jornada* (*Masiosare*, no. 364), 12 Dec.

Pérez Arce Ibarra, Francisco (1999) *La jurisprudencia y la libertad sindical* (Mexico City: Dirección Ejecutiva de Estudios del Trabajo, Secretaría de Gobernación).

Poder Ejecutivo Federal (2009) 'Decreto por el que se extingue el organismo descentralizado Luz y Fuerza del Centro', *Diario Oficial de la Federación*, 11 Oct., pp. 2–5.

Preciado, José Luis (2011), 'El Partido Verde Ecologista: un negocio de familia', *Revista Yucatán*, 11 Nov. 2011 (www.revistayucatan.com/v1/2011/11/11/partido-verde-ecologista-un-negocio-de-familia/).

Quiroz Trejo, José Othón (2004) 'Sindicalismo, núcleos de agregación obrera y corporativismo en México: inercias, cambios y reacomodos', *El Cotidiano*, no. 128 (Nov.–Dec.), pp. 7–17.

Ramírez Sáiz, Juan Manuel (2003) 'Organizaciones cívicas, democracia y sistema político', in Alberto Aziz Nassif (ed.), *México al inicio del siglo xxi* (Mexico City: Editorial Miguel Ángel Porrúa), pp. 133–82.

Raphael, Ricardo (2007) *Los socios de Elba Esther* (Mexico City: Planeta Mexicana).

Ravelo, Ricardo (2006) 'Narcomenudeo en el hospital La Raza' (http://hemeroteca.proceso.com.mx/?p=219937).

Rendón Corona, Armando (2005) *Sindicalismo corporativo: la crisis terminal* (Mexico City: Universidad Autónoma Metropolitana-Iztapalapa/Editorial Miguel Ángel Porrúa).

'Report of the International Trade Union and Parlimentary Leadership Delegation to Mexico' (2009). Document.

Reyes del Campillo, Juan (1990) 'El movimiento obrero en la Cámara de Diputados, 1979–1988', *Revista Mexicana de Sociología*, vol. 52, no. 3, pp. 139–60.

— (1996) 'La representación política en la Cámara de Diputados', in Juan Reyes del Campillo (ed.), *Modernización política en México: elecciones, partidos y representación (1982–1994)* (Mexico City: Universidad Autónoma Metropolitana-Xochimilco), pp. 139–76.

Roberts, Kenneth M. (1998) *Deepening Democracy? The Modern Left and Social Movements in Chile and Peru* (Stanford, CA: Stanford University Press).

Rodríguez, Arturo (2010) 'Pasta de Conchos: el estado, culpable', *Proceso*, no. 1747 (25 Apr.), pp. 37–8.

Rueschemeyer, Dietrich, Evelyne Huber Stephens and John Stephens (1992) *Capitalist Development and Democracy* (Chicago: University of Chicago Press).

Salas, Carlos P. (2010) 'Ocupación, desocupación, ingresos y condiciones de trabajo en México.' Unpublished manuscript.

Samstad, James G. (2002) 'Corporatism and Democratic Transition: State and Labor during the Salinas and Zedillo Administrations', *Latin American Politics and Society*, vol. 44, no. 4, pp. 1–28.

Sánchez, Julián (2003) 'Dicen adiós a la FSTSE', *El Universal*, 6 Dec. (www.eluniversal.com.mx).

— (2010) 'CNTE: buscan acallar rechazo a enlace', *El Universal*, 6 Apr., p. 32.

Sánchez, Virgilio, and Benito Jiménez (2010) 'Parten en Oaxaca a Nueva Alianza', *Reforma*, 29 June, p. 8.

Sánchez Díaz, Sergio (2002) 'Los socialistas y los sindicatos ante el nuevo siglo (el caso de la Coordinadora Inter-sindical Primero del Mayo', *El Cotidiano*, no. 111 (Jan.–Feb.), pp. 81–91.

Sarmiento, Sergio (2008) 'La nota de Napito', *Reforma*, 30 May, p. 1.

— (2010) 'Jaque mate por Cananea', *Reforma*, 8 June, p. 14.

Secretaría del Trabajo y Previsión Social (2010) 'Observaciones del Gobierno de México sobre la queja presentada ante la OIT por la Federación Internacional de Trabajadores de las Industrias Metalúrgicas (FITIM) que alega violaciones a la libertad sindical y protección del derecho de sindicación (caso no. 2694).' Document.

Secretaría del Trabajo y Previsión Social and Comisión Nacional de los Salarios Mínimos (2010) 'Evolución del salario mínimo real'. Document.

Sklair, Leslie (1993) *Assembling for Development: The Maquila Industry in Mexico and the United States* (La Jolla, CA: Center for U.S.-Mexican Studies, University of California, San Diego).

Smith, Peter H. (1979) *Labyrinths of Power: Political Recruitment in Twentieth-Century Mexico* (Princeton, NJ: Princeton University Press).

Stallings, Barbara, and Wilson Peres (2000) *Growth, Employment, and Equity: The Impact of the Economic Reforms in Latin America and the Caribbean* (Washington, DC: Brookings Institution Press/United Nations Economic Commission for Latin America and the Caribbean).

Tribunal Internacional de Libertad Sindical (2011) 'Resolución 2011' (www.tribunaldelibertadsindical.blogspot.com).

Tuckman, Jo (2011) 'Scandal Erupts Around Union Chief in Mexico', *The Guardian*, 8 July, p. 28.

Urquidi, Víctor (2003) 'Mexico's Development Challenges', in Kevin J. Middlebrook and Eduardo Zepeda (eds.), *Confronting Development: Assessing Mexico's Economic and Social Policy Challenges* (Stanford, CA: Stanford University Press/Center for U.S.-Mexican Studies, University of California, San Diego), pp. 561–76.

U.S. Department of Labor (2010) *Status of Submissions Under the North American Agreement on Labor Cooperation (NAALC)*, Division of Trade Agreement Administration and Technical Cooperation, March (www.dol.gov/ilab/programs/nao/status.htm).

USLEAP (U.S. Labor Education in the Americas Project) (2010) *Newsletter*, no. 3 (Fall).

U.S. National Administrative Office (1998a) *Public Report of Review of NAO Submission No. 9701* (Washington, DC: Bureau of International Labor Affairs, U.S. Department of Labor).

— (1998b) *Public Report of Review of NAO Submission No. 9702* (Washington, DC: Bureau of International Labor Affairs, U.S. Department of Labor).

— (1998c) *Public Report of Review of U.S. Submission No. 9702 Part II: Safety and Health Addendum* (Washington, DC: Bureau of International Labor Affairs, U.S. Department of Labor).

— (2000) *Agreement on Ministerial Consultations: U.S. NAO Submissions 9702 and 9703* (Washington, DC: Bureau of International Labor Affairs, U.S. Department of Labor).

— (2007) *Public Report of Review of Office of Trade and Labor Affairs Submission 2005–03* (Washington, DC: Bureau of International Labor Affairs, U.S. Department of Labor).

Valdés Ugalde, Francisco (1994) 'From Bank Nationalization to State Reform: Business and the New Mexican Order', in Maria Lorena Cook, Kevin J. Middlebrook and Juan Molinar Horcasitas (eds.), *The Politics of Economic Restructuring: State-Society Relations and Regime Change in Mexico* (La Jolla, CA: Center for U.S.-Mexican Studies, University of California, San Diego), pp. 219–42.

Valenzuela, J. Samuel (1989) 'Labor Movements in Transitions to Democracy: A Framework for Analysis', *Comparative Politics*, vol. 21, no. 4, pp. 445–72.

Vargas Guzmán, Reyna (2001) 'La representación corporativa en las elecciones federales durante la consolidación del período neoliberal', *Revista Estudios Políticos*, no. 26 (Jan.–Apr.), pp. 229–57.

Vargas Márquez, Wenceslao (2006) 'SNTE y PRI: el voto del magisterio', *Milenio* (Veracruz), 29 Oct. (www.wenceslao.com.mx/sindicato/sntepri2006.htm, accessed 10 June 2010).

Vázquez Trujeque, Eduardo, and Adrián Vizuet Nava (2002) 'Vías para convertir a LyFC en una entidad rentable y de calidad mundial.' Unpublished manuscript.

Velázquez, Mario (2010) *Seguros de desempleo y reformas recientes en América Latina* (Santiago, Chile: Comisión Económica para América Latina y el Caribe).

Vergara, Rosalía (2005) 'Abascal, el fracaso', *Proceso*, no. 1477 (20 Feb.) (online edition).

— (2006) 'Grupo México, poder en Los Pinos', *Proceso*, no. 1538 (23 Apr.) (online edition).

— (2010) 'No pasará', *Proceso*, no. 1744 (4 Apr.), pp. 36–8.

Visser, Jelle (2006) 'Union Membership Statistics in 24 Countries', *Monthly Labor Review*, vol. 129, no. 1, pp. 38–49.

Von Bülow, Marisa (2010) *Building Transnational Networks: Civil Society and the Politics of Trade in the Americas* (New York: Cambridge University Press).

Williams, Heather L. (2003) 'Of Labor Tragedy and Legal Farce: The Han Young Factory Struggle in Tijuana, Mexico', *Social Science History*, vol. 27, no. 4 (Winter), pp. 525–50.

Williams, Mark Eric (2001) 'Learning the Limits of Power: Privatization and State-Labor Interactions in Mexico', *Latin American Politics and Society*, vol. 43, no. 4, pp. 91–126.

Williams, Natara (2005) 'Pre-hire Pregnancy Screening in Mexico's Maquiladoras: Is it Discrimination?' *Duke Journal of Gender Law and Policy*, vol. 12 (Spring), pp. 131–52.

Wionczek, Miguel S. (1967) *El nacionalismo mexicano y la inversión extranjera* (Mexico City: Siglo Veintiuno Editores).

Zapata, Francisco (1986) *El conflicto sindical en América Latina* (Mexico City: El Colegio de México).

— (2006) 'La negociación de las reformas a la Ley Federal del Trabajo, 1989–2005', *Foro Internacional*, no. 183 (Jan.–Mar.), pp. 81–102.

Zazueta, César, and Ricardo de la Peña (1984) *La estructura del Congreso del Trabajo: estado, trabajo y capital en México* (Mexico City: Fondo de Cultura Económica).

Zepeda, Roberto (2011) 'The Decline of Trade Unions in Mexico during the Neoliberal Period.' PhD thesis, Department of Politics, University of Sheffield.

INDEX

INSTITUTE FOR THE STUDY OF THE
A M E R I C A S

The Institute for the Study of the Americas (ISA) promotes, coordinates and provides a focus for research and postgraduate teaching on the Americas – Canada, the USA, Latin America and the Caribbean – in the University of London.

The Institute was officially established in August 2004 as a result of a merger between the Institute of Latin American Studies and the Institute of United States Studies, both of which were formed in 1965.

The Institute publishes in the disciplines of history, politics, economics, sociology, anthropology, geography and environment, development, culture and literature, and on the countries and regions of Latin America, the United States, Canada and the Caribbean.

ISA runs an active programme of events – conferences, seminars, lectures and workshops – in order to facilitate national research on the Americas in the humanities and social sciences. It also offers a range of taught master's and research degrees, allowing wide-ranging multi-disciplinary, multi-country study or a focus on disciplines such as politics or globalisation and development for specific countries or regions.

Full details about the Institute's publications, events, postgraduate courses and other activities are available on the web at www.americas.sas.ac.uk.

Institute for the Study of the Americas
School of Advanced Study, University of London
Senate House, Malet Street, London WC1E 7HU

Tel 020 7862 8870, Fax 020 7862 8886,
americas@sas.ac.uk
www.americas.sas.ac.uk

CPSIA information can be obtained
at www.ICGtesting.com
Printed in the USA
LVOW12s0244180616

493134LV00001B/33/P